5 MINUTES

to

BETTER BRANDING

Bite-Sized Bits of Marketing Wisdom

ROB WEINBERG

author of Ask Mr. Marketing

Rob Weinberg
PO Box 1681
Carlsbad, CA 92018
(858) 774-2420

rob@marketbuilding.com
www.askmrmarketing.com

Published by Write Away Books, USA

WRITE AWAY

BOOKS

Taking Authors From Idea to
Manuscript to Marketplace ™

writeawaybooks.com

PO Box 1681
Carlsbad, CA 92018

Print ISBN: 979-8-9896431-0-3
e-book ISBN: 979-8-9896431-1-0

This publication is designed to provide accurate and authoritative information with regard to the subject matter covered. It is sold with the understanding that both the author and publisher are not engaged in rendering legal or accounting advice. If legal advice or other expert assistance is required, the services of a competent professional person should be sought.

—From a *Declaration of Principles* jointly adopted by a Committee of the American Bar Association and a Committee of Publishers and Associations, and only changed a little bit.

Front cover: 5-Minute icon designed by Ylivdesign

Get the newest **Ask Mr. Marketing** columns at
askmrmarketing.com

Sign up for a free monthly marketing newsletter at
https://bit.ly/mbtsignup

Connect on LinkedIn: https://linkedin.com/in/robweinberg

Connect on Instagram: https://instagram.com/askmistermarketing

This book is available at quantity discounts for bulk purchases or
promotional applications. For information, contact
rob@marketbuilding.com.

Visit our exciting small business marketing website at
www.marketbuilding.com.

Also by Rob Weinberg

The Ultimate Guide to Pedestrian Polo

Removing the Mystery from Marketing

Streetwise Internet Business Plan

To Randy Rose, who encourages me, puts up with me, and still laughs at my jokes after all these years. Because this was all your idea in the first place.

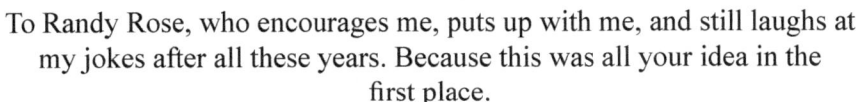

To Emily Weinberg, who challenges me, makes me laugh, and provides me with a steady stream of baked goods. You've expanded my creative flow . . . and my waistline.

And to my furry companion Buddy who, though gone, is never forgotten.

Contents

Acknowledgments

There are WAY too many people to thank for this volume becoming a reality. I wish in particular to show my appreciation for my bride, Randy Rose, for her insights, stamina, and nonstop abilities to make me see the world in a different way. Her unstinting support over the years continues to make ALL the difference in my life.

Also to be recognized are Steve Dreyer (*Pomerado Newspapers*) and Jordan Ingram (*Coast News*) for being great editors, wielding their red editorial pens like a scalpel in the hands of a fine surgeon; Trudy Armstrong of the San Diego Foundation for helping to turn an idea into reality; Chris Belden of Oregon Health Science University for her proofreading skills and never-ending common sense; my entire virtual Rolodex of friends and colleagues upon whom I periodically call for feedback; and the readers who have taken the time over the years to provide comments and criticism that help me to constantly improve my craft.

Finally, a note of appreciation to Jennifer Geist of Open Books Press, who walked with me and held my hand the last few steps.

And, of course, none of this would have been possible without the help of Bob Yehling, Erin Jenkins, and Danielle Tweedy at Write Away Books. You guys are amazing, and I look forward to working with each of you every day for a long time to come.

It ALL Started with a Hat!

Since 2018 I've belonged to a business support group called Chair-men's RoundTable. I sit on the board, attend most meetings, and actively participate. They know me for the hat I always wear.

I knew I'd gone too far the day I was at an organizational meeting and the chair called for committee reports. Seeking mine, she looked straight at me, sans hat, and asked "Where'd he go?"

She wasn't kidding, either. Of course, the moment I put the hat on she recognized me. "Perhaps," I wondered "perhaps I've over-branded myself."

It's easy to get lost in any crowd, and many people go to great lengths to avoid being forgotten. Coloring your hair purple, sporting facial tattoos, or wearing large green shoes all help one stand out.

For me it's a hat. Not a baseball cap, mind you, but a hat. A REAL hat. A Panama hat, demonstrating both style and personality. And it DEFINITELY helps me stand out.

Let me start, though, with a confession: I never liked wearing hats. The hat hair, the hassle, what do you do with it when you're not wearing it . . . these were the kinds of issues that made the concept of a hat seem like more trouble than it was worth to me.

Then I moved to San Diego and was quickly persuaded of two things:

- New Yorkers don't acclimate well to chronic sunshine, and
- Guys without much hair need hats to prevent getting a sunburn.

A trip to New Orleans in 1994 convinced me that the panache of a Panama hat was the solution that suited my style, while keeping the sun off my receding hairline. I started wearing it periodically, but still saw it as equal parts nuisance and benefit.

The value of the symbiotic relationship with my hat was proven at a chamber of commerce event. Understanding that wearing a hat indoors or at night is considered rude in some circles, I had left the hat at home.

Imagine my surprise when the executive director yelled at me, "How can I introduce you as the man with the hat if you don't wear your hat?"

Point taken.

Soon thereafter, the larger value of the hat as a marketing tool was driven home to me as I attended a wedding. There, an attractive woman called to me by name, generating the fish-eye from my bride and a blank stare from me.

Nope ... I couldn't place her face. "You spoke at a seminar I attended in March," she smiled "and I remembered you because of your hat."

Almost unintentionally, the hat had become my personal brand. And over time I've come to wear it day and night, inside and out, practically every day of the year. I'm currently on my 18th one, and must replace them every 18–24 months.

And no, they're not always the same style ... though they're typically pretty close.

This consistency of personal branding has ensured I'm recognized by friends and strangers alike, both up close and from a distance. Those who see this or a similar chapeau think of me ... even if I'm actually hundreds of miles away.

I'm obviously on their minds.

And so, the hat has risen from being a mere fashion accessory to being the focus of my personal branding campaign. From a strict marketing perspective, that makes it invaluable.

Despite the arguable rudeness of wearing a hat indoors and/or at night, the chronic presence of my straw topper consistently ensures I can be noticed instantly in any group setting. Inside, outside, daytime, and night, the hat is now an extension of my personality, as well as being the very personification of my brand. It appears in my newsletter, social media, logo and elsewhere.

This consistent branding with the hat helped persuade the *Pomerado Newspaper* chain—a division of the *San Diego Union Tribune*—and the *Coast News* and others to have me write a weekly advice column called Ask Mr. Marketing.

And what began as a brief experiment in July 2006 has evolved into a significant vehicle responsible for training thousands of professionals and nonprofessionals alike in the many ways that marketing impacts their daily lives.

You'll find a healthy sample of these columns between these pages. And while the marketing topics covered in the column vary from week to week, I've focused these dozens of columns strictly on personal and organizational branding. Other marketing topics—sales promotion, public relations, strategic planning, etc.—will be addressed in future volumes in this series.

And yes, you CAN read any of these articles in five minutes or less.

I've spent my career tearing down the curtain of mystery that so many needlessly hang around a simple process of communicating why someone should work with them. Which boils it all down to this: If you're looking for common-sense marketing solutions, solid nuts & bolts tactics, and easily understood implementation, you've come to the right place.

And if you've got marketing issues of your own that I'm not addressing here, come visit me at askmrmarketing.com. Not only will you find my newest columns posted every week (for free!), but you can also send in your own questions and I may be able to help.

Because, as you'll see by reading this book, the answer's probably easier than you realized.

So take five minutes and read one of these columns. Or whip right through and read the whole thing in about three hours. Either way, by the time you're done, you're sure to know a little bit more than when you started.

With that said, I wish you a week of profitable marketing...hopefully helped and encouraged by this collection of experience, insight, and bad jokes.

Good luck!

Thanks to Stella Wilner

A little background of who I am and how I got here may help to explain my creative bent and my sometimes-quirky approach to the world at-large and communications in particular.

First, let me introduce you to the scrawny kid with the glasses and braces.

Yes, that's me in the corner: a first grader overshadowed by a narcissistic father, intimidated by school bullies, and overwhelmed by . . . well, everything.

I cried a lot in those days, and buried myself in the school library reading everything in sight. It was a safe and quiet environment where nobody bothered me, and I was left to explore fantasies of being happy and having more friends than just my family's dog.

Only anyone starting life this way needs to find some way to express themself. Fortunately, Stella Wilner—my first-grade teacher—encouraged me to write stories as a way to escape my daily troubles. In hindsight I came to see her wisdom, providing me with a harmless outlet while keeping me both out of trouble and harm's way.

The very real fact that my scrawling was indecipherable didn't seem to bother her. It was *so* bad that Sadie Waters—my third-grade teacher—likened my handwriting to ". . . dipping a chicken in an inkwell and scratching it across a piece of paper."

Maybe I should have become a doctor?

Regardless, Mrs. Wilner encouraged me, guided me, and showed me the value of writing, libraries, networking, and public speaking. She provided the pressure valve a lonely youngster needed, helping me become a productive member of society, rather than acting out on the frustrations being heaped upon a sensitive child.

And so I wrote about anything and everything, dumping my juvenile thoughts onto paper as if I were Ernest Hemingway. And yes, most of it was *terrible*!

My aunt, Pearl Slater, played an equally big role in shaping my life when, on my 13th birthday, she gave me a copy of the book *Why a Duck?* This volume presented the funniest scenes from the Marx Brothers' movies. To that point I'd never heard of this anarchic gang of comedians, and I was enthralled to see Groucho—all of 5'7 ½"—putting oversized bullies and troublemakers in their place with a few well-chosen words.

And while I first thought everything he and his brothers did was scripted, a little fast research uncovered how much of their humor was ad-libbed. So I studied and parroted Groucho carefully, calculating that few of my tormentors would be familiar with his material. Then, sensing potential for all kinds of success, I immersed myself in the works of Milton Berle, George Burns, and Don Rickles, harvesting and cribbing good verbal put-downs from them and every other wise guy I could find.

The results were miraculous, and I realized the power of the well-placed word or a sharp retort could quickly put me above those who ruled with their fists.

Guided by a mother destined to become a world-class sculptor, my creative side flourished. And with basically no friends until I hit 10th grade, I spent countless hours fending off the obnoxious and putting pencil to paper. Along the way my mother taught me to roll with the punches, greet each day with a smile, and never give up on my dreams. She taught me about having faith in yourself, being honest and loyal, and the importance of being a good friend.

She summed it up in seven words: "It costs you nothing to be nice."

At 15 I met a girl who was pretty, smiled at me, and laughed at my jokes. Imagining myself in love, I married her at 22 and we played house in the nation's capital. There I worked with trade groups, honed my craft, and ignored signals that she was cheating on me. Okay, her "swimming" with her boss every weekend *should* have been the tipoff . . . but I was young and foolish. We divorced at 25, driving into my skull the importance of character; I was one, and she had none.

Fortunately, though, there were no kids. I did suggest we stay together for the sake of the car, but the idea didn't go over very well . . . and we moved on with our lives. I finally connected all the dots when she married her boss. I'm guessing she cheated on him too.

Connecting the dots became a theme for me personally and professionally. It was the concept that permanently changed my future when I moved to New York to work in sales promotion for my father. For though I'd have been very happy as a lobbyist or political operative, he had other plans and manipulated me to join his sales promotion agency in the Big Apple. There I learned to run a business, got a marketing degree to complement the one I had in political science, and got training in public speaking. I also learned some important lessons while working with some high-level clients, including:

- KLM Cargo, for whom we developed a vehicle discussing their services, the 79 countries they flew to, and the reasons one should do business with them. Without the internet or easy ways of customizing marketing materials, we delivered gorgeous custom binders with the initials of each recipient emblazoned on the cover. The bookkeeping was nightmarish, but the results were outstanding.

  LESSON LEARNED: Personalization in marketing is terribly important!

- Ringling Brothers, who wanted "a marketing adventure" to announce their headquarters' permanent relocation to Winter Garden, Florida. Our plans to deliver a custom book and an individual tape recorder to each member of their audience was scuttled due to budgetary concerns.

  LESSON LEARNED: Money's important. Reality sometimes gets in the way of creative deliverables.

- Schieffelin & Co., for whom we were doing a steady stream of collateral materials for the various brands of spirits they were importing. On my first day on the job I was handed a printed catalog and asked to read it before it shipped to the client. Turns out there was a typo (the client's name was misspelled), and I was told I'd probably just saved the account.

LESSON LEARNED: Details matter!

My years in New York can be summed up as a great education. Indeed, if you ignore the need to chronically sublimate my personality to help my father achieve his own vision of financial success, everything was perfect. Only I'm not the kind of person who thrives on every relationship being transactional, and I chafed within the straitjacket I'd allowed myself to be placed in.

━━━━━━━━━━━━━━━━

Then there was the night I attended a Mets baseball game. Riding home on the subway, I encountered a friendly face with a nice smile and gobs of freckles. I offered to play connect the dots with her freckles, and the rest (as they say) is history.

Yes, yes . . . you can read the entire tale in the personal branding section. Did you *really* think I'd leave you hanging? And this young woman, soon to be my bride, helped me come to recognize the most important questions one should be asking at the outset of any marketing or branding discussion:

- What's your objective?
- Who's your audience?
- How will you define success?
- What's your timeframe for success?
- What resources are you willing to invest?
- Why should someone buy from you?

The freckles scenario demonstrated to me that these questions apply to business and personal communications alike. She—and they—would guide me from that day forward.

━━━━━━━━━━━━━━━━

Combined with the lessons I'd learned working for my father, I was seasoned by the time I hit 32 and left New York, first for New England, then Southern California. Over the intervening years I deepened my knowledge base, using it to expand market share for various employers by an average of 500 percent before hanging out my own shingle.

Of course, smart marketing also means knowing what *not* to do. Consider the jewelry manufacturer who contacted me in June 1999, inviting me to his factory for a day's consulting. Y2K—the turning of the millennium—was happening six months hence, and the owner spent four hours showing me an idea he had for a commemorative paperweight he wanted to manufacture and sell.

After he finished his presentation, he asked my opinion. "Don't do it," I advised. He was livid, screaming at me about how I didn't know what I was talking about and how dare I and such. Finally he caught his breath and asked what prompted my outrageous conclusion, and I told him the following:

1. He only had a prototype. Production of deliverables, including packaging, probably wouldn't be ready until August. As there were thousands of similarly themed products already on the market, getting shelf space on such short notice would be difficult at best.

2. He had no marketing budget. This meant he'd be relying on the kindness of editors for free press. As publications generally need long lead times, editors would be working on year-end issues by the time he had products ready to show them … and *everyone* would want to be in those issues.

3. Everything he would be manufacturing would be obsolete in seven months. "Turn it into an annual fundraising tool for a fraternity and it's a different story," I suggested.

Then this gent snarkily told me every one of his employees had loved it. "What do you have to say about *that*?" he sneered. I only had one question: "Who signs their paycheck?" Obviously, when the boss shows you something and excitedly reports, "This is my new product idea," few will suggest anything other than support, lest they lose their job.

The result: He angrily tossed me out of there, paid my bill, and stopped communicating with me … for six months. That was when he sent me a note saying "You saved me $350,000 that day. I didn't do the project."

Another lesson on what not to do: Don't jump the gun. I learned this one when I got a phone call from a friend about a noted local restaurant that had gone out of business. The owners had never marketed themselves, didn't join any networking groups, had an attitude problem, and closed during the week between Christmas and New Year . . . which would otherwise have been one of their biggest weeks.

So their corporate demise made sense to me. To confirm, I tried calling them (no answer) and visited their (disconnected) website. My conclusion: The call was accurate.

I promptly wrote an article excoriating them for their marketing transgressions and basically saying they got what they deserved. Only 10 minutes after I posted the article online (and it was already on press for distribution on the street), I got a note from a friend that the restaurant was, in fact, open.

OOPS! I immediately corrected the story online, wrote a retraction to be published in the next issue of the weekly newspaper I wrote for, and tracked down the restaurant owner to explain the situation and how I'd make right on my mistake.

Yeah, *that* was a fun conversation!

The result: The added publicity gave the restaurant the best week they'd ever had. Yet despite the obvious lesson here (visibility is good for business), they still handled their communications as usual and eventually closed up shop. However, I had the lesson reinforced regarding the importance of doing your homework more thoroughly.

Today I am married to the world's greatest (and most patient) woman. We have an amazing daughter (an up-and-coming opera star), a happy home, and (you knew we'd get there eventually) ongoing inspiration that led to this book.

Living three miles from the beach in Southern California, I've earned the respect of the community, learned to focus on what's truly important in life, and genuinely like myself. And I've learned to observe people and situations with a constant eye out for the bullshit factor.

No longer do I allow myself to be bullied into accepting someone else's biases, hatreds, and weaknesses as my own. And this revelation, fed by a chronically supportive network of family, friends, and fans, has encouraged and consistently reinforced my ability to spot ways of communicating better.

It's a talent that my clients, associates, and interns regularly benefit from.

And as you absorb these gleanings from my first four decades in the marketing communications industry, I am hopeful you'll take several lessons of your own away, including:

- Grammar and spelling still matter. I know that suggesting that makes me a dinosaur, but I have always rebelled against my then six-year-old daughter's argument that "I can spell words any way I want to." To me, the answer is "Not if you want others to know what you're talking about."

- Facts matter too. Just having an opinion doesn't make it so, and if you want to persuade others to your way of thinking, you'd better be able to make a compelling argument. Yes, I know in these days of political flim-flammery that isn't always true. There's *way* too much tendency to trash the competition, trying to bring them down rather than making your own argument.

- Get your facts straight. All around us are daily examples of lies, half-truths, incompetence, and manipulation. Each should remind you of the importance of talking straight. As we say at Rotary International, the first question is "Is it the truth?"

  And while I have no objection to legitimate benefit comparisons, I'm not a fan of just tossing bombs. It may work in politics, but doesn't (and shouldn't) apply in marketing. Because as I consider the sixth important question—Why should someone buy from you?—I know that merely saying "I'm the best in the business" isn't going to persuade anyone to buy from you ... unless you can back it up with facts.

  All of which boils down to this: If you're good at what you do, tell your story and the people you want to be doing business with you will see it for what it is.

These are the philosophies you'll see as you read through my columns. They reflect strategies I employ daily, melding the good and the bad and putting it all to use to generate unique marketing solutions and profitable results for a wide range of industries and nonprofit organizations.

And now, as a marketing consultant, author, and managing partner of Write Away Books—Taking Authors from Idea to Manuscript to Marketplace™—I'm looking forward to sharing more of it with you.

Join me at askmrmarketing.com and follow my continuing adventure. Because the fun is really just starting . . . and it would be a pity if you missed any of it.

Rob Weinberg
November 3, 2023

The Values of Branding

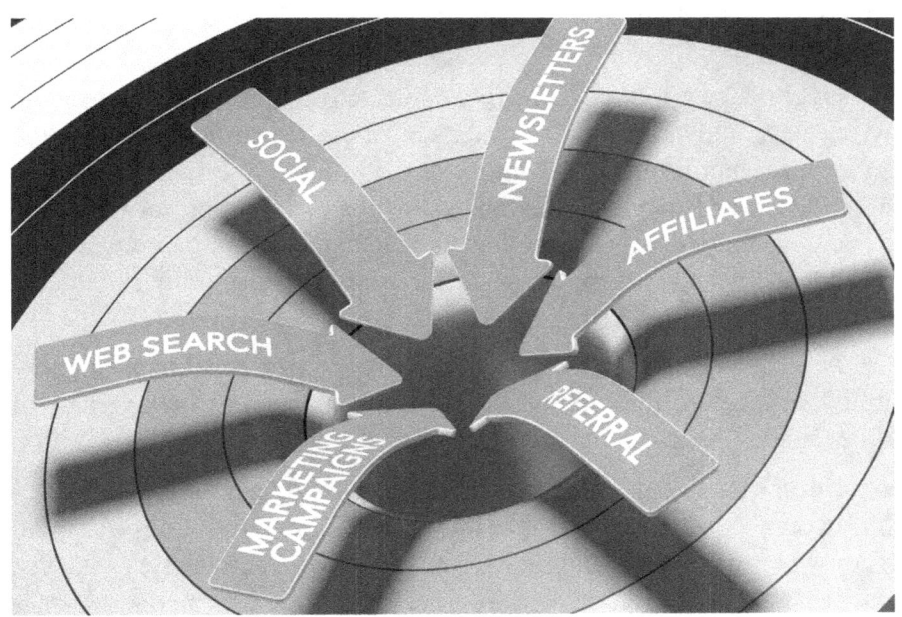

Why Bother Marketing?

O kay, let's get to the guts of it: Is it *really* necessary to market your business?

Over the past four decades I've come across many arguments about why you should or shouldn't market a business. Regardless of the industry or size, the discussion always seems to line up the same way. Successful business owners talk about the value of investing in their business. Owners who are scrambling for a toehold in the marketplace see marketing and advertising as an unnecessary expense, rather than as a critical investment in their company's future.

Arguments for marketing include increasing profits, increasing visibility, and controlling the message. Arguments against include lack of time, lack of competition, and controlling the budget.

But the reality is that many small business owners see the marketing budget as a piggy bank that they can raid anytime times get tight. They won't necessarily cut their own salaries or entertainment budgets, but will spend less on advertising, networking, social media, or sales promotion.

The problem, of course, is the moment you reduce your overall level of marketing, your visibility (obviously) goes down. This, in turn, leads to a loss of business, which generates lower budgets and ... well, you get the idea.

Still, many people just don't get it. They see their marketing budget as a tempting target they can just apply straight to the bottom line. One gentleman recently told me of his marketing budget being slashed by 65 percent because company costs were too high compared to revenues. Rather than using the already budgeted funds to attract more customers, his board of directors cut the very lifeblood needed to expand the company.

Their action is guaranteed to have the exact opposite result!

Still, the question remains: Do you really need to market your organization? And the answer *must* be a resounding "*Yes!*" Not because I make my living by developing and providing good marketing, but because *you* do. And to prove my point, I'd like to share this simple tale:

THE HOT DOG STORY

Once there was a couple struggling to make a living with their hot dog stand by the side of the road. Trucks and cars would whiz by without even a glance, despite the fact that their hot dogs were fresh and tasty and their coffee was the best in the entire area. It was very difficult to support themselves and their young son.

One day the wife got a bright idea. "Why not market ourselves? We can put up a big sign and also put our message on billboards. We can even spend some money on the local radio stations extolling the virtues of our great food."

Before they knew it, trucks and cars were stopping by and business was booming. They enlarged the stand and hired many people to accommodate the traffic. They stayed open seven days a week, 24 hours a day and made more money than they ever thought possible. It was the American dream come true.

Business stayed good and they grew the business into a chain. Eventually, their son grew up and went to college. He studied hard and earned a degree in economics. His delighted parents took him into the business with a fancy title and office to match.

Their clever son studied the general business conditions and surveys of the future by the most reputable people in the nation. He finally concluded: "We are headed for a recession, and possibly a depression."

He discussed this with his parents and convinced them that his training would now pay off. "Let's stop advertising and save the money, and when things change we'll be in good shape again."

The signs came down, radio commercials stopped and trucks and cars whizzed by as they did before the company started promoting. Business worsened, with the chain dwindling back down to one stand. Finally, bankrupt, the last stand was also shut down.

As the father sat with his wife one hour before closing for good, he couldn't help but think to himself: "My son was really right: We *are* in a depression."

Moral: **You can't sell it if you don't show it or tell anyone about it.** It's been proven again and again that those who market when business conditions are slow are *way* ahead when it gets better.

━━━━━━━━━━━━

There is no clearer way to say it. If you don't tell your story—and tell it well—everything else falls apart. Prospects won't know what you make, so they won't buy it. If they don't buy what you're selling, there'll be no floors to sweep. No need to buy coffee cups. And no invoices to send out. All those annoying things you have to deal with will go away, because your organization won't exist unless you let people know you're there and open for business.

Put another way, without your marketing (and the requisite second half: the sale) you're guaranteed to have *nothing*.

━━━━━━━━━━━━

FOOD FOR THOUGHT: The best reason for advertising today is the sale you'll make tomorrow. There is always a tomorrow to prepare for, more competition coming down the road, and seeds that need to be planted to grow your bottom line.

250,919,240 Marketing Messages

Consider how hard your marketing will have to work in the next 12 months.

The US Census Bureau reports today that the average American adult will live to be almost 78. And, in case you were wondering, that does take into account any ground lost due to COVID-19.

Now consider that every adult over age 18 is exposed to as many as 10,000 marketing messages *every single day!*

If that's surprising, think about your typical day. You see TV ads, newspaper coupons, business card logos, desk calendars, websites, and direct mail. Then there are the product labels, clothing labels, and store-front signs.

The list is truly endless.

As a point of reference, in the mid-seventies the average person was on the receiving end of between 500 and 1,600 marketing messages per day. Most of these ads were on billboards, in newspapers and magazines, and on television or radio.

By 2007, that number had risen to 5,000 and (though there are no official figures), it seems to have doubled again.

This latest increase, of course, is courtesy of the internet in general, social media in particular, online gaming, and our fixation with computers, phones, and distractions from daily life. The addition of commercials to streaming TV has only made the situation worse.

Naturally, as each new form of technology evolves, the world's advertisers look for ways to exploit it in spreading their particular message.

Admittedly, most of these messages are both subtle and forgettable. You probably don't even realize you're being marketed to when you see a car logo on the rear end of the vehicle ahead of you on the highway. And we all ignore those product placements in movies and TV shows, right?

The point is, it's not easy for marketing professionals to be heard above the din. Here's what you're up against to get your business noticed and remembered these days. (This is when we get to do a little math. I know: math. UGH! But stay with me for a moment.)

Assume a child under age two sees no advertising at all. It's a false assumption, of course, but I need to start this conversation someplace. At two, product impressions leak into that child's life at a rate of 300 impressions daily. At three it's almost 1,000; at four, 1,700; and so on until maxing out at 10,000 every 24 hours by this young adult's eighteenth birthday.

Let's see ... carry the two ... let me take off my shoes to count my toes ... this means if I've done my math correctly, this child has already seen an astonishing 28.1 million marketing messages ... give or take a dozen. Sixty years later it's risen to a mind-numbing 250,919,240.

And yes, that did account for leap years.

Holy socks! That averages out to one marketing impression every ten seconds of this person's entire life ... including when they're asleep!

Obviously, competition for today's consumer's attention is merciless. Marketers must invest money and time to be noticed. New messages need to be constantly tested to beat the other guy to the sale. Others are constantly tweaking strategies, seeking methods for stealing the customer out from under their competitor's nose.

And anyone not working daily to improve their business withers and dies. Guaranteed!

Got a headache yet? Take a break to catch up on your reading. Here are two books you'll probably find helpful for inspiring your creativity:

- *A Whack on the Side of the Head*, with dozens of exercises in the art of being more creative; and
- *Purple Cow*, a *Wall Street Journal* bestseller about transforming your business by being remarkable.

Both books will shake cobwebs from your head and improve your thinking process.

With each new day comes new opportunities, and this year won't be any different. Resolve now to think creatively over the next four quarters. Make the most of every business opportunity coming your way.

And whatever you do, do *not* get complacent, hoping that whatever you've done in the past will continue to work for you. Because there are thousands of reasons why someone won't pay attention to you every day, and any businessperson thinking "It's worked for me in the past, so I'm sure it will work for me in the future" is doomed to failure.

FOOD FOR THOUGHT: The average American adult is exposed to roughly 10,000 marketing messages every 24 hours. Any business hoping to break through that noise had better have a good strategy.

Making the Most of Your Marketing Materials

===

Whether you're selling products or services, you always want to convey an image that doing business with you is a pleasant experience.

One of the best ways to do this is with coordinated messaging across your marketing platforms.

For those unfamiliar with the message process, it's helpful to consider in advance the key components: copy, design, and graphics.

There are multiple places where you're going to tell your story. The most common are a website, social media, text, and email—all digital, and all easily, quickly, and inexpensively changed when need be.

But what happens if you also need a business card, brochure, flyer, poster, or banner? These are all printed, and can't be changed as quickly or inexpensively as your digital media can be.

Now consider using sales promotions, publicity, and direct mail. Or television, billboards, radio, or other broadcast media.

Each level of messaging has its own criteria for implementation and success. Professionals who know how to write or design for print may not be appropriate for broadcast or websites. And most folks don't realize that copy, design, and graphic needs change from one type of messaging tool to another.

In short, marketing is never a one-size-fits-all proposition.

So before you start organizing your next branding campaign, consider the following:

- **COPY.** People don't read much anymore, so fewer words are usually better. This means making sure every word counts. When editing, think how you'd get your message onto X (formerly Twitter).

- **DESIGN.** The borders, shapes, and colors used around and behind the copy help you break up your paragraphs and make your words more readable. Don't fear white space.
- **GRAPHICS.** A picture is worth a thousand words. A video is arguably worth *much* more!

In every messaging tool, you'll need to combine these three components (copy, design, graphics) to suit your audience and whatever you're selling. A BMW deserves gloss and full color; a box of pencils requires simple black and white. Use enough words to accurately tell your story, along with a pleasant design and that graphic image.

Simple, right? But did you realize that every marketing effort requires many decisions? For example:

- **USING SPACE WISELY.** You're creating a business card. Do you get the standard size (3.5" × 2") that everyone is used to? Too many words mean you'll need to use a smaller font. Or you can get a larger card that customers won't "get." Or you can put those words on the obverse side—valuable real estate that most folks leave blank.
- **DON'T DO IT YOURSELF.** Unless you're a professional designer, writer, or photographer, bring in the pros. Don't think that because you know everything about making hats, you should be able to market them too. Your job is making the hats; their job is to promote the hats.
- **WATCH YOUR BUDGET.** Photographers and illustrators come in many flavors, including professional, college student, and strawberry. Someone just starting out can give you great quality without charging much. Review lots of portfolios, and you may find a diamond in the rough.
- **CONSIDER RENTING.** You can rent an image from iStock or Shutterstock for a few dollars. Just be sure to acquire it in the highest possible resolution so you have the option of using it in other media. Image resolution can easily be scaled down and still look good, though you cannot take any image in low resolution and make it look good in print.

There's also a potential risk from renting photos, as it may show something similar to what your competition is presenting.

Pay attention to what others in the marketplace are doing to avoid this problem.

- **USE ILLUSTRATIONS.** They can be less expensive than having original photography created, but have similar issues: professional vs. student, renting vs. buying, using images similar to what competitors use.
- **BE CONSISTENT.** The types of words, graphics, and images that you use should be consistent across all your marketing. It's not just the tagline that makes up your brand, but colors, fonts, shapes, design, and overall tone.

Good writer/designer teams can help you get by without photos or illustrations. A top-notch designer can take good copy and make graphic elements (shapes, colors, fonts, white space) look very appealing ... and without royalty worries.

Finally, here are a few professional hacks that may be of some value to you:

- Hiring a model generally means paying royalties every time the ad appears. This can add up over time.
- Buying the photo outright costs more than renting it. Do it only if you plan to use those pictures a lot.
- Have the model *and* the photographer sign a release that *you* own the photos.

FOOD FOR THOUGHT: Consistency across marketing platforms is critical, and the criteria you're using for your overall branding needs to be used by every team of writers and designers to ensure your look and tone remain in place at every level.

One Firm with 23 Images

The whole concept of branding is simple: Create a visual (character, colors, logo, etc.) that instantly generates an image in customers' minds. Seeing it reminds them who you are, what you do and sell, and the experience you offer to bring to them every time you and they interact.

When repeated regularly, that image creates an emotional response from your customer.

It's why someone who sees McDonald's golden arches immediately thinks of fast food, Ronald McDonald (their clown mascot), and consistent menu choices and quality at every location.

Now it's true that the McDonald's restaurant in Sedona, Arizona, has turquoise arches, due to local zoning issues. It is both an anomaly and a tourist attraction.

However, if other restaurants in this chain had blue, green, or purple arches, rather than the traditional gold, the company would lose the consistency that customers count on, albeit subconsciously.

Other businesses follow similar rules. For example, imagine you're shopping at Target, whose colors are white and red. Wander into any of their locations and you'll see the same colors, the same logo, and invariably, Bullseye the dog.

But what if you walked into the toy department and the walls were painted yellow? And the floor in home furnishings was green. And you were surrounded by black displays in the automotive section.

Kind of destroys the "one store" experience, doesn't it?

I recently encountered the lack of consistency issue at a local real estate brokerage. Twenty-three in-house realtors had their business cards at the front desk, and each had a different look.

Which means these realtors were voluntarily relinquishing the marketplace strength they'd have had by keeping their branding consistent.

All of them needed to use the same business card template, the same colors, and the same tagline.

But no … these 23 realtors were all over the map. With business cards printed on a computer, the owner didn't set a good example. Reproduction quality was poor on his cards, the type was tiny, and his photograph was unimpressive. Rather than demonstrating the quality he wanted, he offered excuses.

As they say in Portugal, "A fish stinks from the head down."

When I asked him about the firm's branding, he was more concerned with the few dollars he saved by buying his business card stock at Staples. The obvious problem, of course, was his cards looked like he'd printed them himself … and this doesn't do much to instill a feeling of success amongst would-be clients.

His team members weren't much better, with cards printed in various shades of blue. They had inconsistent layouts, and an incredible number of typographical errors in job titles, names, phone numbers, and email addresses.

From thereon it was the wild, wild West. Every card was different; every shade of the rainbow appeared in abundance. Many of these team members used their own taglines instead of the company's line. Photo usage was spotty, and one picture looked like the woman's head had been clamped in a vise.

And did I mention the realtors who used their own logos instead of the company's? It was, to put it politely, a hot mess.

Erratic branding of flyers, brochures, and business cards is something typically encountered at startups, volunteer organizations, and nonprofits. These are the kinds of folks who feel they have no time to invest in their branding, and are either unwilling or unable to set aside an adequate budget to have someone else create one for them.

But if you want to be thought of as a truly professional marketer, investing in steady branding is a *must*!

This is why Coke, which designs ad campaigns to suit local community style, still always uses the same logo, font, and colors.

And it helps explain why FedEx has the same imagery on trucks, packaging, and forms, even as their colors change for each service they sell.

None of this is accidental. Solid, consistent branding takes a lot of commitment, planning, work, and money to reinforce the image in consumers' minds over a period of years. A refusal to invest the time, money, and brain power is an invitation to failure.

Not surprisingly, the realtor in question above asked how he could grow his business. I was reminded of *The Sound of Music*, in which Julie Andrews said that the beginning is a very good place to start.

Which is what I advised to this gentleman . . . and would say to anyone concerned that their bottom line isn't growing fast enough. Revitalize your corporate image, then keep your branding consistent throughout the rest of the company. Be sure all employees' presentations match, and remember: This is *your* company, not theirs.

And if your employees have a problem with the philosophy of brand consistency, then perhaps they're not the right employees for you.

FOOD FOR THOUGHT: No business, individual, or nonprofit *ever* got into trouble by having consistent branding.

Big Image. Big Mistake?

===========

My ex-wife used to tell me that size really matters, while I regularly maintained that it was the amount of fight in the dog, rather than the dog's size, that made the difference.

Of course I was talking about competition in business, though I've got a sneaking suspicion she was referring to something else. However, since I haven't spoken with her since 1985, we'll never really know, will we?

Still, this discussion *does* present an important question: Should you change your company name to appear bigger?

Before doing anything, consider your marketing objectives and whether appearing big (message: "We deliver more!") or small (message: "We're efficient and personal") better suits your individual and professional style.

And given the legal, financial, and communication investments needed to rebrand a company, think long and hard before you proceed down this path.

Then, if you decide to move forward, remember that your company name speaks volumes about you, your ego, your business's personality, your customer, and your product line.

All of which combines to mean you'd better have a serious understanding in advance of your customer profile and the image you want to portray.

Let's take my friend Bernard Michaels, for example, who is considering a rebrand of his two-person firm. He's currently debating several options, including:

- The sense of personalized owner-attention coming from "The Bernard Michaels Company."
- A name like "Michaels & Associates," imparting the message "customers meet the owner, then work with an assistant."

- "Michaels Manufacturing," suggesting belching smokestacks ... and all that that implies.
- He could even appear to be *really* big by calling his business "Michaels Global Industries."

Which strategy is best? It depends on whom you ask.

As a partner in a two-person marketing agency, I've always been partial to telling folks upfront that we're a small company that delivers personalized attention, value-added services, and profitable results. It seems to work for who we are, eliminates questions, and is both honest and straightforward.

Yet I'm unquestionably missing out on some *very* big conversations and potential deals. Prospective clients know my firm is small and don't typically bring me big deals because they figure I can't handle them. And even though I can put together a team that *could* handle bigger deals, they don't invite me to the big kids' table.

So in this regard, yes, a bigger name would be beneficial. Changing your company's name would make your business appear bigger. It'll also change expectations of you from both customers and other industry players.

Because if you go for the bigger name at your own company, the law of unintended consequences could deliver to you prospective customers expecting you to fulfill that huge image you've created. And unless you have financing and infrastructure (or alliances) in place to ensure you can deliver on promises you're making—directly or indirectly—you may end up disappointing a lot of people and losing more than you gain.

And remember what Mom always said, "You only get one chance to make a first impression."

Though it may seem quaint these days, I believe you should live up to the commitments you make. Companies like IBM represent themselves as big, but also deliver big. If you can't deliver on your promises, there's little advantage to making yourself seem bigger than you really are.

Which kind of brings us full circle back to the original point of this branding conversation (and no, I see little benefit in resurrecting the discussion about my ex-wife): Go ahead and change your company name if you think there's a benefit to the exercise. Just be sure to remember what you're selling, to whom you're selling it, and how you're going to deliver on the image you're projecting.

=====

FOOD FOR THOUGHT: Your company name speaks volumes about you, your ego, your business's personality, your customer, and your product line. Change your company name if you think there's a benefit to the exercise.

Who Really Cares about Your Name?

In 2008, at the height (or depths) of the biggest financial crisis in 70 years, JP Morgan Chase & Co. acquired all deposits, assets, and certain liabilities of Washington Mutual Bank.

Washington Mutual (WAMU) had been the nation's largest thrift at that point, and they vanished virtually overnight with the Chase "merger." Branch names and persona changed in the blink of an eye, and it was like WAMU had never existed.

Coincidentally, at the same time the Rancho Bernardo (CA) Joslyn Center renamed itself the Ed Brown Senior Center at Rancho Bernardo.

Why did either of them do it? Rebranding can be challenging, problematic, expensive . . . even risky. There's always the chance you'll lose customers amidst the turmoil.

Still, there are plenty of real-world examples of companies that have made that leap and come out as a winner. Some have been looking to maintain a healthy, dynamic brand. Others seek to reinvent their business after a crisis.

Interested in the thinking that goes into the rebranding process, I tried reaching out to JP Morgan Chase. However, unable to find anyone beyond the janitor willing to take my call, I instead spoke with Arlene Cawthorne, then executive director at the newly named Ed Brown Center.

"Community leader Ed Brown was responsible for our very existence when he got the center built in 1989. We felt it was time to thank him," she explained.

Fair enough. Vital to North County's senior social/educational experience, the center's classes and services enhance lives for people either just entering or already in their golden years, and all without taxpayer support. Their interest in expanding market visibility by tying in with a local community leader is completely logical.

Rebranding hits the reset button on your marketing, offering you the opportunity to start fresh with your customers. Sometimes it works, like when Taco Bell switched its personality from chihuahuas to being more of a cantina.

Sometimes, like when Facebook rebranded as Meta or Twitter became X, it leads to a collective shrug.

Instagram may get the prize for most effective rebrand of the past few years. When they unveiled their new logo, some loved it, some hated it, but everyone was talking about it and had an opinion.

Which is exactly what a good rebrand is *supposed* to do!

Of course, most businesses don't have the resources to do a significant rebrand like Taco Bell did. It's hard work developing a new company name, logo, tagline, color palette, font, website, social media, and collateral. And it's not something that one should do frivolously since existing brands have equity.

Furthermore, amidst the confusion caused by a rebranding effort, there's a risk that competitors will peel off some of your customers. Forgetting the old company even existed is not unusual.

This probably explains why organizations large and small all use their moment of public prominence to restructure their respective offerings. New services and products are introduced, and the new brand needs to be simultaneously introduced using social media, publicity, websites, and every other communications tool at your disposal.

Depending on how big your own company's image needs to be when rebranding, you may also want to throw in some TV commercials, newspaper ads, sales promotions, or direct mail along with new signage, brochures, and forms to re-create your public appearance.

And, as was said of the Volvo rebrand of 2021, it should pay homage to the past while looking forward to the future.

Meanwhile, back in Rancho Bernardo, the Ed Brown Center is transforming itself with loads of hoopla at a grand opening ceremony. They'll follow this fun event and a bunch of publicity with a revitalized website and newsletter. The new canopy's already been installed.

Bottom line: Even if you're not facing a global rollout (and the subsequent critique of a brand identity refresh), it's important to unveil your rebrand correctly. Don't handle it frivolously, as this is the company's equity that's at stake. Build your team with the right people, and bring them into the process early.

Once the rebrand is finalized, unveil it to your internal team with all the flash you usually reserve for the public, and make sure your new brand assets are easily accessible. That way you get the full team's buy-in, and everyone can start putting them to use immediately.

Then remember that rebranding campaigns mean working very hard to retain current customers. People typically don't like change, so altering a professional image means providing increasing reasons customers shouldn't wander away.

Finally, if you're considering a rebranding effort for your own organization, plan it carefully and thoroughly. Bring in the pros to do the heavy lift of creative and implementation. Allow enough time and money to do things right. And be sure there's potentially a big payoff for the investment.

You'll be happy you did.

FOOD FOR THOUGHT: Use the opportunity when rebranding your business or nonprofit to introduce new services and products. Use every communications tool at your disposal, and make as big a splash as possible.

Does Your Name Really Matter?

I'm a *big* fan of old movies. I find many of the films from the thirties and forties to be *far* superior to most of what's out there today. The earlier movies had style—making their points without foul language, nudity, explosions every few minutes, or computerized technology. They instead relied on wit and nuance, lighting and camera angles, costumes and locations.

To me, there's nothing better than a rainy day spent watching Humphrey Bogart or Katherine Hepburn on TCM. When my daughter told me her favorite movie star was Jimmy Stewart, it felt like a watershed moment.

Which brings us to last night, when I watched *In Name Only* with Cary Grant. I love Cary Grant, and have found his roles to usually be very well defined. He's been a newspaper editor (*His Girl Friday*), archaeologist (*Bringing Up Baby*), and cat burglar (*To Catch a Thief*).

In fact, in almost all of Grant's 73 film roles we know what he does. Yet, with the movie *In Name Only* he runs Richard Walker & Company . . . and never identifies what the firm makes or sells. Even IMDB is stumped, merely referring to him as wealthy.

As I watched the film, I considered the company name. Of Mr. Walker, one must assume he purposely left his company's goals mysterious. Perhaps he's involved in nefarious activities. Maybe he's confused . . . or just has a big ego.

I'm guessing the latter.

An organization's name can be critical to its success. Buying a company means owning the inventory, real estate, website . . . and name. Using a business's branded name ensures you'll more easily maintain existing customer relationships.

But having a company whose name doesn't tell you what they do does little beyond feeding the owner's ego.

Which brings us to a basic question: What's your objective? Assuming your objective is to sell products or services, having a name that illustrates what you sell seems to make the most sense. It puts it right up front, and mitigates consumer confusion while eliminating the need for questions.

Names like Unicorn Jewelry and 5-Star Auto Repair are obvious. Names like Macy's are not.

Sure, Macy's runs the Thanksgiving parade and anchors practically every shopping mall in the country. Everyone knows they're a department store, right? Only it took decades for that awareness to sink in to the general consciousness, and at a cost of many millions of dollars.

Most businesses aren't willing or able to invest that much money to build a relatively generic name into a market force. However, they can short-circuit the process by making their name straightforward and simple.

Now consider your company name. Regardless of what you sell, would a stranger take one look and understand the business you're in? If not, I'd argue that your organization doesn't have a good name.

Jones Legal Services makes good marketing sense. Jones Corp. doesn't.

True, there are ways around this challenge. Mel Johnson's Carpet Sales & Service works from both marketing and ego standpoints. But what happens when Mel is out of the picture, either because he sells the business, dies, or is incapacitated? When the XYZ Corp. buys Mel's business (and brand name), they'll need to spend a year or two presenting both names together, side by side, to ensure customers get used to the idea of the new ownership. Then, when Mel's name eventually vanishes (which is virtually guaranteed), XYZ's name will still be recognized and accepted by longtime customers.

Not convinced? Still insisting on naming the company merely to satisfy your ego? It's okay by me, but you'd better plan to have a robust marketing budget for promoting yourself and building recognition. You're going to need it.

Or you can just help yourself by creating a clever, straightforward name that tells the world what you do ... without questions.

FOOD FOR THOUGHT: If someone's feeding their ego, naming the company after themselves makes perfect sense. However, those wishing to actually sell stuff should rethink that strategy.

Having a Character Working for You

A fter 40+ years in business, I have yet to meet a CEO who doesn't want to make their organization more visible.

The thinking is simple: More visibility leads to more revenue. As circus magnate P.T. Barnum once observed, "Without publicity a terrible thing happens: nothing."

And it's true that with markets increasingly homogenized, marketplace visibility has become a *big* problem. The average American adult is on the receiving end of almost 10,000 marketing messages *every single day*. Franchises, chains, and big box stores spend massive amounts supporting their images and trademarks.

Breaking through the clutter is, at best, a significant challenge.

Being heard above the din requires some kind of consistent messaging that's creative, clever, and different. Smaller firms and independent brands *can* still win in this kind of overloaded environment by creating a proprietary character to represent their company.

It might be a cartoon or flesh and blood—human, animal, or invention. But regardless of the form it takes, these creations all represent their sponsor and their customized message, typically with humor or irreverence. The one consistency throughout: always keeping an eye toward pushing the envelope a bit to ensure they're heard.

Breathing life into such a fictional representative increases chances a business will be remembered when it comes time for someone to make a purchase.

Products with personalities have become a part of our collective culture. In my head, I still hear Mr. Whipple saying, "Please don't squeeze the Charmin!" even though the commercials stopped in 2000 and actor Dick Wilson died in 2007. His consistent (and comforting) presence in over 500 television commercials probably had something to do with that.

And who over age 50 could forget Charlie the Tuna? Madge the Manicurist? Or Fred, who awakened daily at 4:30 to make the donuts? These people became like old friends, still reminding us of our favored products of days gone by.

Creating a brand's personality can be as simple as licensing someone else's creation. For example, Time Warner used to "hire" the Warner Brothers' Road Runner to represent their broadband service with the same name. MetLife hired Snoopy and Woodstock (of *Peanuts* fame) for decades to pitch their insurance products.

Yet merely slapping a picture of SpongeBob SquarePants onto your storefront won't make you stand out. Especially if the guy at the other end of the street has done the exact same thing.

And believe me: There's nothing worse than investing in licensing a character to market yourself, only to find your closest competitor has licensed (or knocked off) something similar.

Which brings us back to developing a unique product image for your business, and some things to consider, including:

- Will it be a real person or an animation?
- What kind of personality and message will this character project?
- What audience will this character appeal to?

These are the kinds of questions Progressive Insurance addressed when creating Flo. They're also the kinds of issues Write Away Books is focusing on as they explore converting the image of one of their founders into a cartoon character.

However, let's all learn a lesson from Esurance. The online insurance company created Erin, the pink-haired secret agent, and encouraged consumers to "own" the brand. However, as CBS News reported, "many consumers decided they wanted a piece of the Erin brand, and the results had nothing to do with cut-rate third party, fire and theft policies. If you do a Google search for 'Erin Esurance' you'll see that it prominently returns X-rated pictures of the star that 'fans' have created, some with a remarkable degree of verisimilitude to the real thing."

OOPS!

Here's the thing, though: Once you've done your up-front strategizing, using a character (living, animated, computer-generated, or Claymation) as your marketing icon is easy. And, provided you maintain control of them, they can oftentimes say the kinds of things you'd like your representatives to be able to say, but can't for some reason.

Yup, even characters with attitude (consider Morris the Cat) can succeed. Indeed, as a recovering New Yorker, I'm partial to characters with attitude, but ... well, New York, don't you know?

Success down this road comes from creating the right mascot, infusing it with the proper personality, and committing enough time and money to allow a following to develop. So once you've decided to travel this path, incorporate this character into your website, social media collateral, digital ads, and every other communications vehicle and format in which you're active.

Because properly developed and supported, an imaginary figure can demonstrate all the great things about whatever you're selling. It will make your company memorable and has potential to significantly increase your sales for years.

Just don't forget to call the trademark lawyer ahead of time to protect your investment.

FOOD FOR THOUGHT: Breathing life into a fictional representative increases chances a business will be remembered when it comes time for someone to make a purchase.

The King of Taglines

In 2009, George "King" Stahlman marked the end of an era in San Diego's marketing world when he died of emphysema.

Universally recognized for his jingle—"It's better to know me and not need me than to need me and not know me"—Stahlman actively promoted himself to the top of the very competitive bail bonds business.

He was well respected by those around him, with a reputation as a person who did whatever he could to help out anyone in need. At this writing, years after his passing, King Stahlman's face, name, and tagline have become part of the vernacular of the local business community.

Between his business's founding in 1946 and his passing 63 years later, King Stahlman thrived through seven recessions. His business philosophy was simple: "Early to bed, early to rise, work like hell and advertise." Stahlman also had the oldest bail bond license in the state, and for decades his company was one of the best-known firms in San Diego County.

Mr. Stahlman was an excellent example of how any business can benefit from a good idea, hard work, some imagination, and a well-conceived and solidly implemented marketing plan.

And, regardless of what you sell, his example should be making you wonder how your own business can benefit in the long run if you market more. Because whether the economy today is good, bad, or somewhere in-between, it's worth pausing to examine your own marketing efforts to chart a more successful course moving forward.

The thing is, when the economy is good many businesses attribute their success to their talent, even if they don't deserve such credit. They may just be benefiting from general economic conditions or shortages they had nothing to do with.

In other words, they may be in the right place at the right time.

And when things get rough, many of these same firms will pull in their horns to save money on their marketing. This, of course, is actually the exact time when they should be investing *more* to get the word out and expand their customer base.

Operating from a position of fear is a surefire strategy for eventually closing your business and working for someone else. As my old friend Bob Culkeen used to say, "You can't live your life by always asking 'What if?'"

Refusing to invest in your marketing budget (or slashing it when things get rocky) not only hurts your market presence, such activity also leads to management making questionable decisions like cutting customer service departments and sales staff at the very time when the company needs to be boosting those resources.

The domino effect of such poorly considered decisions can easily threaten a firm's very existence. Business owners in such a state of mind will reflexively ignore opportunities available from spending a few dollars on Google ads, newspaper coupons, or other relatively inexpensive media.

True, a focus on social media can help your budget, provided you're working with existing in-house resources. But far too often, social media has you talking to your existing audience without opening new doors. Even posting to chat groups and hashtagging the heck out of every story can have limited impact.

Meaning you're putting all your eggs into that one basket, and by its very nature you'll limit your results.

Even worse, you're probably overlooking other free and inexpensive marketing opportunities sure to increase visibility and the bottom line, like:

- **Networking.** Chamber of commerce event attendance potentially exposes your product or service to hundreds for mere pennies.
- **Improved website presence.** Free, regularly updated online content and blogs will lure more visitors.
- **Public relations.** Newspapers may be cutting back, but they're still interested in real news.

- **Email blasts.** Your in-house database is a great resource for reminding everyone your business is still around to serve their needs.
- **Public speaking.** Persuade sales prospects by the dozen—and they'll even feed you.
- **Drip campaigns.** They help wear away reasons someone won't do business with you.

Just as you'd never build a house without a blueprint, your marketing plan will help ensure you have a strong, solid future for your business. It'll examine where you and the economy are at today, where you want to be in five years, and how you're going to get there.

Because, even if there are storm clouds on the horizon, things will improve one day, and every business needs to plan now for then.

As the old saying goes, "The best reason to market today is the sale you're going to make tomorrow."

After all, King Stahlman was successful for over six decades by increasing his company's marketing in bad times. The man obviously knew something so many of the rest of us ignore, and we can all profit by following his lead.

FOOD FOR THOUGHT: There's never a downside to consistent and clever promotion of your business.

Eight Weeks of Free Marketing

Many businesses and nonprofits give away a range of advertising specialties with their name on it. The hope (and expectation) is that the buyer or consumer will remember the organization's name the next time a particular product or service is needed.

Truth be told, my life is an amalgam of advertising specialty items. Shirts, hats, thumb drives, clocks, shopping bags, and a wide assortment of other knickknacks fill my home, car, and office. It is literally impossible to turn in my little world without bumping into a handful of goodies given away by one organization or another.

And it makes sense on a basic level. Consider, for example, the printed calendar I have on my desk from Streeter Printing. Consciously or subconsciously, I see it 20 times every day. Which is why I automatically think of Streeter when I need any type of professional printing services.

Coincidence? I *think not*! This cause and effect undoubtedly explains why so many office workers use coffee mugs from the local accountant or pens from their dentist's office. The accountant and dentist are both trying to stay top of mind with a gentle prod when the competition is (hopefully) nowhere in sight.

And it's highly unlikely you'll ever walk down the street without seeing someone wearing a T-shirt from the local bank, grocery store, or pizza shop. These promotional tools are relatively inexpensive to purchase, and can be produced quickly in a variety of styles and colors. This combination of ease and low cost makes their distribution and use to willing customers too tempting to ignore for most firms and organizations.

But the smartest folks in the crowd have a brand that's *such* a must to own that customers happily pay for the right to sport the name and/or logo.

Before dismissing my theory, see if your wardrobe includes at least one item with a sports team's name on it. How about that shirt from the last rock concert or beer event you attended? And don't forget the buttons, bumper stickers, and hats from political campaigns you've donated to.

Driving down the road in San Diego, I regularly see license plate holders announcing alumni from all the area colleges. Those premiums are distributed to donors to the annual fundraising effort.

Which brings us to Bob Worner, a Rancho Bernardo, California–based car broker. Because for the past two months, I've been providing him with free marketing services.

Bob's a good guy, and I believe him to be both honest and honorable. He has spent years providing new and used vehicles for less money or hassle than if you purchased them from your local dealer.

I also admire his business model: unlimited inventory, extensive product knowledge, great customer service, fair pricing, and a well-deserved reputation for quality.

Naturally, when my 15-year-old Saturn bit the dust, I called Bob. He made the process painless by asking me a few questions, guiding my purchase, arranging for a test drive, and bringing my new car to my door 48 hours after I'd initiated the first conversation.

Yet I noticed that my new car was delivered without license plates. Unknown to most people, the California Department of Motor Vehicles has 90 days to send those plates to a new owner. In the interim, Bob installed promotional license plate frames and paper license plates promoting his company.

It was a perfect marketing opportunity … and for the next eight weeks I became a mobile billboard for Bob's company. If you think about it, I actually paid him for the privilege without getting anything further in return.

This was nothing short of brilliant!

True, I could have removed Bob's promotional materials when I got home, but distractions and inertia combined, resulting in my failure to act. It's like journalist/cartoonist Allen Saunders said, "Life is what happens to us while we are making other plans."

This inertia was obviously what Bob was counting on and, from a marketing perspective, I must respect that. Furthermore, if I'm being totally honest, I'd have probably done the exact same thing if I were in his position.

Therefore, the next obvious question becomes: How do you get someone to pay you lots of money and willingly help promote your business?

You could be a nonprofit organization which solicits money from sponsors, then puts those sponsors names on a shirt and sells those shirts or gives them to paying event participants. Almost every marathon and beer festival follows this model quite successfully.

Or you could build the proverbial better mousetrap. Take Starbucks, as an example, which sells roughly 5 million cups of coffee—*coffee!*—each day through its company-operated stores (which are about half their total locations). They then encourage customer loyalty by enrolling them in a rewards program (13 million+ active members) who get to earn drinks, food, Delta SkyMiles (another rewards program encouraging customer loyalty), signature cups, accessories, and . . . well, you get the idea. And every time the customer sees that cup, they're reminded to return to Starbucks for all the other trinkets.

Branding your organization so strongly and positively that everyone wants to be associated with your success results from a combination of quality, fair pricing, hard work, consistent messaging, and commitment of time and money.

And making those investments with an eye on long-term benefits can earn you rabid fans happily buying from you just so they can say they did.

It's a pretty slick trick when you think about it. And it gives the rest of us—those who aspire to be like Starbucks—something to strive for.

FOOD FOR THOUGHT: How do you get someone to pay you lots of money and willingly promote your business?

I Pledge Allegiance to This Logo . . .

A donkey, an elephant, and Santa Claus walk into a bar . . .

The obvious joke here isn't that elephants and donkeys drink in bars (though that *would* account for Santa's red nose!), but that the chances of getting a Republican and a Democrat to agree on almost anything—including which bar to drink in—becomes more remote by the day.

Courtesy of cartoonist Thomas Nast, the donkey and the elephant have become symbolic of America's political parties, and Santa universally represents the Christmas holidays. Nast's imagery from the late 1800s is recognized around the world to this day.

Now, for good measure, let's add a cross, a six-pointed star, an angel blowing a trumpet, a crescent and star, and the atomic whirl into the conversation.

Representing Christianity, Judaism, Mormonism, Islam, and Atheism (respectively), these symbols are not the beliefs themself, but icons that believers (or nonbelievers) use to identify themselves, each other, and their generalized philosophies and views of the world.

Each of these symbols have become a type of shorthand you can easily grab onto. From a marketing perspective, they're logos.

A logo is meant to evoke an emotional reaction to a product, service, or idea with a simple image—like a glass of beer, a pretty girl, a sexy car, or an imposing estate.

A picture is supposed to be worth a thousand words, and both religious and political symbols certainly qualify.

But how does one determine the "best" logo? Target's target, Nike's swoosh, McDonald's arches, and FedEx's hidden arrow all jump to mind. Other types of images also generate an instant recall and emotional response.

Take flags, for example. Their single image (or sometimes just the colors) can spark feelings of pride, love, and belonging. They can also instill anger, frustration, and a certain level of isolation.

Nothing seems to accomplish these feelings more effectively than the American flag.

American ideals, when competing in the global marketplace, need an easily understood image representing them. This flag provides that image, helping "buyers" to rally around and justify their purchase.

Like Pepsi's globe, the American flag appears on clothing, jigsaw puzzles, pens, and coffee mugs. It pops up on vehicles, in television commercials, and gets used by others hoping to ride the American "brand" to their own financial success.

After years of broad-based visibility, the Stars and Stripes have saturated the world market. Seeing it creates instant feelings of loyalty for (or against) its mission statement.

The American flag makes millions get a lump in their throats. It wordlessly evokes responses the original copywriters and designers would be proud of. The taxes we pay are royalties for using their intellectual property.

Comedian Stan Freberg's 1996 CD about Jefferson, Madison, and Franklin running an ad agency to market America for client George Washington had a media campaign, flag logo, and a real-life Uncle Sam, combined to sell the US like a bar of soap.

Not coincidentally, political campaign slogans like Ronald Reagan's "It's Morning in America" do the same today. Perhaps that's why, when the Iraq war began, the White House appointed an advertising czar to help sell our message overseas.

Rarely is the word logo applied to political party mascots, religious symbolism, or flags. Lofty words like patriotism, values, and love are bandied about, but I maintain these are the reactions one hopes to see generated from the image . . . but are not the images themselves.

This is important to consider as you're assessing your own organizational branding and marketing results. If your logo gets customers and public dialogue whipped up, and/or instantly brings your company name, values, and purpose for existence to their minds, then it's arguably doing exactly what you want it to do—attract attention, remind people that you're there, and reinforce the message that they should buy from you when they're ready to make a purchase.

However, if your logo looks just like someone else's, then it's reasonable to ask why someone should remember you instead of the other guy.

Because, like all marketing messages, the important thing is to make yourself stand out from the crowd today, and to be memorable in the long-term.

Finally, based on the amount of branding impressions, effectiveness in broadcasting its message, and ability to evoke emotional responses across the spectrum, the American flag gets my vote for most effective logo in the world.

—————————————————

FOOD FOR THOUGHT: Find a symbol to represent your brand. Present it to your audience. Repeat daily.

My Biggest Marketing Pet Peeve

The most heinous marketing mistake is arguably open for debate, though I would maintain it's typographical errors. They surround us and are easily avoidable . . . especially in these days of spell-checking programs and artificial intelligence (AI).

Of course, those programs are a significant part of the problem. If a sentence needs *two*, *to*, or *too*, all three may be spelled correctly . . . but it's the context that makes all the difference.

For this issue I place the blame squarely at the feet of disconnected parents and students focused on computer screens. After all, logically, you're more likely to absorb proper grammar and word usage if you're actually reading it.

Most people are reading less these days, minimizing the chance they'll spot spelling mistakes without mechanical aid. (For example, how many people read this column? Is there anybody there? HELLLOOOOO!)

But I digress. Making a mistake is one thing, but failing to correct it is another story altogether. And it's inexcusable when these mistakes appear in marketing materials being actively used to persuade prospective customers to buy a product or service.

Here's a good example of not proofing one's work. I recently visited a drugstore near my home. Outside was a display of plastic porch furniture with a sign that read (I'm not making this up):

Managers special

Outdoor Furniture

Includes Swings, Beches, Gazeebos, Chairs, Etc. 50% off

Without much trouble I spotted three mistakes in those 12 words. "Manager's special" was missing an apostrophe, "Benches" was missing an *n*, and "Gazebos" had one too many *e*'s. My 10-year-old spell-check program immediately picked up all three errors, making me wonder whether the store's manager needs a pair of reading glasses from aisle seven.

My wife says I'm a pain in the neck when it comes to this sort of thing. Okay, truth be told, my wife says I'm a pain in the neck about lots of things, but particularly about all the typos I find around me. Perhaps she's right.

But I consider it offensive to my intelligence to find a fine restaurant's menu riddled with misspelled words. Actually, typographical errors just jump off the page at me from menus at every level of dining, though I'm much more likely to be forgiving of a cafe than a hoity-toity establishment.

It's why I like eating at restaurants where the menu is written in a foreign language . . . so I can relax without knowing if there are typos right in front of me.

And it's not just menus! Billboards, brochures, websites, emails, and PowerPoint presentations are regularly chock-full of words spelled incorrectly and/or used improperly.

Now I don't mean to suggest my work is perfect. I'm more guilty than most of writing the way I speak. Words like "and," "but," and "I" too often start my written sentences. And I constantly ignore the lesson attributed to Sir Winston Churchill about not ending a sentence with a preposition, to which he purportedly responded, "That is something up with which I will not put."

There are even people who don't like my writing style (can you believe it?), thinking it's either too kitschy or too highbrow (depending on the personal style of the critic du jour). The occasional typographical error has escaped my word processor, and friends have gleefully pointed out my mistakes.

Yet the drugstore situation (remember the drugstore situation?) convinced me that marketers mangling language is the way of the future, only trumped as a linguistic concern by the thought that so few customers seem to notice the mistakes.

SIGH!

Admittedly, guys like me—people who insist words be spelled and used correctly—are dinosaurs. Look no further than today's email, brimming over with run-on sentences and words crying out for proofreading, for evidence that both good grammar and proper spelling are dying arts.

And I won't even begin to discuss the emails with phrases like "I 8 2day," which I, in my curmudgeonly state, would insist should read "I ate today."

Conclusion: Preventable mistakes in marketing materials send the message that the marketer doesn't care about the organization's image, craftsmanship, quality, or customer. They're disrespectful to the supplier and the clientele. And consumer ignorance is no excuse for sloppy marketing.

A six-year-old using a calculator rather than learning the multiplication tables is doomed to use that calculator as a crutch throughout life. Writers using spell-check or AI from an early age also have a crutch. Remove the computerized spell-check and automated thesaurus from someone who is linguistically handicapped, and their writing takes on a certain misspelled sameness.

And be honest—will signage announcing "You should buy our grate stakes because they taste grate" really make you want to buy steaks?

From both a marketing and a societal standpoint, there's no downside to communicating well and spelling words properly. Why wouldn't you want people to think you're intelligent and methodical enough to double-check your own work?

Here's the bottom line: Build in extra time to double-check your work for mistakes and you'll appear more professional. Period!

Have someone else check it for you too. After all, if you made the mistake once, you may make it again when you reread your work. In my case I have four sets of eyes (besides mine) look at every column before it's published to ensure clarity of message and lack of typos.

I also read all final drafts out loud to make sure they sound right. Oddly enough, this strategy also increases the chances I'll see if something is wrong.

Finally, send your own message by refusing to do business with companies that can't get their linguistic act together. They're insulting *your* intelligence if they can't take an extra minute to see if they're selling gazebos or gazeebos. Their prices may be 50 percent off, but that doesn't mean the buying public needs to mark down its intelligence level.

─────────────────

FOOD FOR THOUGHT: Build in extra time to double-check your work for mistakes and you'll appear more professional.

Stop Selling for Yahoo

My friend John Jones and I have an ongoing debate.

John's company, Jones Manufacturing, has a website (jonesmanufacturing.com). John has an email account through them (john@jonesmanufacturing.com).

John uses his business address sometimes, and it's printed on his business card.

Yet he insists on using an email address of johnjjm@yahoo.com for the bulk of his business-related email. I believe he's making a mistake.

My friend's had this free account for years. He claims Yahoo's ability to store his old emails is preferable to the space taken up on his server by years of archived emails.

And I get where he's coming from. As a pack rat, I save every email related to every project I'm working on. Most of them also end up in the archives when a project ends, perhaps never to be looked at again.

Meaning if an assignment is lengthy, complex, or both, there's a lot of email to hang on to. This leaves you with five options:

1. Clean house and ditch the old emails;

2. Store them all in your email folder, which can seriously slow down your email over time;

3. Store them on your hard drive, which can take up a *lot* of space;

4. Store them on an external drive; or

5. Store it all off-site.

John has opted for door #5, preferring to not have hundreds of emails clogging up his computer system.

And while I understand his point, I still insist that good branding demands he always use an email address with his own company name in it.

The way I see it, every time your email address flashes before a reader's eyes, the return address leaves a subtle marketing message.

Which means even if that email isn't read, an impression has still been made.

Drip. Drip. Drip. Like water wearing away a rock, the constant repetition of your company's name helps wear away reasons why someone won't do business with you. And with enough repetition, at some point the recipient will connect your company name with whatever they need to buy that you are selling.

And they'll (theoretically) contact you to make the deal. This makes at least a modicum of sense, right?

However, if your email address originates from Yahoo, AOL, Gmail, Hotmail, or any other company besides yours, that selling opportunity has been minimized. Because every email received comes from johnjjm@yahoo.com, rather than John@jonesmanufacturing.com. Consciously or not, recipients will think first of yahoo.com.

True, this scenario won't make it harder to spread your message, but it also won't simplify it.

Face it: Every American adult is inundated with so many marketing messages every day that you can't afford to overlook any communications opportunity if you actually want to reach them. Plus we're all finding our customers are numb to our communications efforts, and you need every advantage to try and get ahead.

Or (arguably) just to stay even.

So if you recognize that reality, why would you want to voluntarily throw away the branding advantage inherent in your domain name?

In the movie *Mulan*, the emperor observed, "A single grain of rice can be enough to tip the scale." What if, in the battle for market share, that subtle reminder from your email address is that grain of rice that can tip the scale in your favor? Did you just needlessly lose the battle for the sale because it was easier to just use the free website host?

Okay ... I'll confess I use Yahoo accounts when buying stuff online. These accounts receive most of my junk email. Because I frankly don't care a fig what a spammer or would-be vendor thinks of me. I'm not trying to sell to them, and if they don't like me I'll just go elsewhere.

However, everything related to my business and sales efforts gets branded by my company email. Those emails have signatures with URL, phone, tagline, and social media links. After all, this is my cyber business card we're talking about, and I don't want to miss any openings.

Plus I know that every email and signature I send out into cyberspace could potentially get forwarded to hundreds of other people.

I want *my* email address in all their hands, because who knows what doors it might open?

So, John, while I understand your Yahoo account is free and filters spam from your regular account, I think you're missing a trick when it comes to building your business. Let me again encourage you to brand your own company name on your business emails. It's easy, it's smart, and it's potentially lucrative.

And, if I haven't made my argument clear enough, contact me at rob@marketbuilding.com and we can kick it around further. I'm always happy to chat.

———————————————————

FOOD FOR THOUGHT: Brand your own company name on your business emails. It's easy, it's smart, and it's potentially lucrative.

Marketing and My Dead Dog

===============

I miss my dog Buddy. He left us on July 24, 2019, and he was the sweetest pooch I've ever met.

Buddy had a habit of popping up in this column over the years. As my marketing agency's mascot, he helped put smiles onto clients' faces. He'd review everything I wrote, always provided encouragement, and asked the tough questions.

Occasionally, he would write in asking how he could get me to give him more squeaky toys or snacks. He wasn't exactly known for his subtlety, either!

And now he's gone. Attorney Lance Margolin noted, "To have the love of a dog is truly a privilege. Sadly, their short lifespans must be one of God's crueler tricks."

I concur. Buddy's 14 years with us seemed painfully brief, and his passing was devastating for all who knew him.

And though the easy answer would be to get another dog, it's hard—nay, impossible—to fill the hole left by the death of a loved one.

After he passed, I forced myself to clean out his toys, sweaters, and food from the pantry. There I discovered unopened cans of dog food that he'd shown interest in, only to reject them shortly thereafter.

And while my immediate instinct was to just pitch them or give the unopened cans to a fellow dog lover, I instead found myself in a fog bringing them back to Trader Joe's in Escondido, California. That's when I got a lesson in human kindness, and another on the value of living up to your company's reputation.

For those who don't do their shopping at Trader Joe's, the atmosphere is fairly laid back and the team members tend to be pretty cool people. And upon visiting this particular store, I explained the situation to the manager.

It's also worth noting here that I had no receipt or proof I'd bought it there. I had neglected to bring my wallet, and lacked a credit card or driver's license.

All I had was a dead dog.

Alex took an interest in my story, taking time to look at my pictures. He listened patiently, letting me carry on as long as I needed to, and offered me a box of tissues when my eyes started to leak.

He never questioned me or suggested I was anything other than sincere. Then he took every product I had and reimbursed me with cash. Whether they were bought there or not was unimportant; I was in pain, and he was in a position to help.

In fact, Alex not only reimbursed me for the dog food, but he also personally paid for some flowers for my family.

As they say in New York, he was a real mensch ... an upstanding guy ... and he has my eternal thanks and undying loyalty. Alex helped my family get over a big hump that day, and his gestures had an immense impact on us. I made sure to send a letter about the entire incident to the company's CEO, mentioning Alex by name.

The obvious goal of any business is to be profitable and pay employees a fair, livable wage. To reach these objectives, we advertise, network, promote, and (hopefully) deliver on our promises.

But life should be about more than just making money. And what's sometimes forgotten is that we're all human. We make mistakes, get cranky, miss appointments, or need to be reminded of things.

We also sometimes forget to treat each other with a little extra kindness ... especially when societal pressures encourage us to all be a little colder to each other.

Besides politics or work driving increased hostilities, prompting these issues may be a spousal argument, physical disorder, a sick child ... or an ailing friend.

Regardless of your field, you, too, can be a mensch. Send good wishes if a supplier or a team member gets married or gives birth. Be supportive when someone dies. Provide a compliment and think twice before you make that snarky remark. Remember how you'd like to be treated, and pay it forward.

Moshe Engelberg, author of *The Amare Wave*, regularly reminds us of the importance of introducing love and support in the workplace.

And Alex reminded me that, regardless of your business, each of us sometimes gets a chance to do the right thing for a total stranger. He willingly listened at length to my tale of woe, then chose to bypass short-term profits in lieu of customer goodwill. His decision is guaranteed to be better for the company's bottom line over the longer term.

And his attitude is certain to provide a significant boost to his career through the years.

Management's simple gesture that day—the unquestioned refund and the flowers—has ensured I'll do business at Escondido's Trader Joe's *long* after the event itself is history.

Suggesting that as you think about your own business philosophy, you should ask yourself: Wouldn't it be nice for you to have customers speaking this way about your organization?

FOOD FOR THOUGHT: Remember how you'd like to be treated . . . and pay it forward.

Personal Branding

The Statement Your Car Makes

A few years back I gave my daughter my 2002 Saturn. Now I'll confess that I liked that car because, despite it having 142,000 miles on it, it ran well and was fully paid for. And, given Saturn's reputation for running 250–300,000 miles, I figured there was still a lot of life left in the old girl.

Furthermore, in addition to the car being completely broken in and comfortable to drive, there was the whole car-shopping adventure that I was anxious to avoid.

However, my bride persuaded me that an older vehicle with a few dings and scratches wasn't adequately broadcasting my success. So we gritted our teeth, went through the entire "How much does it cost?" "I can't tell you until you commit to buying it," routine, and came home with a brand-new Honda Civic.

My new car better reflected who I had become. It provided to me steadier wheels while simultaneously reinforcing the importance of public image.

Okay . . . painful as it is, I'll now admit this publicly: my wife was right and I was wrong. Which explains why I'm now tooling around town in a shiny new car.

This experience also reminded me how my mom had regularly admonished me that nobody wants to buy from you when your shoes have worn-down heels or your jacket's fraying. Mom's logic was also sound; they won't do business with you because they feel sorry for you.

A car is both an extension of your personality and a symbol of your success. I mean, let's say you're looking to sell your home and are debating between working with two realtors, neither of whom you have a preexisting relationship with. If you're being completely honest, are you more likely to choose the guy driving the new BMW . . . or the 1973 Pinto?

My experience suggests you're going to be inclined toward the BMW driver every time. Because even if they're equally effective in the marketplace, the image imparted by the BMW suggests to you that this realtor is more successful.

Plus, as Mom (who had *lots* of advice to offer on the subject) used to say, everybody wants to be associated with someone who's successful.

Of course, not all old cars signal frugality or lack of success. You'd probably be jealous if I drove up in a DeLorean. Or what if I picked you up in a 1928 Model A Ford that I was using as a branding tool? I'm guessing it would probably initiate *quite* a conversation between us, at which point you'd probably ask for a ride. Then, being out on the road, there's a good chance that we'd *both* be standing out from the crowd.

Still, the question remains … does driving a Bentley project an image of extreme success, or generate a *Gilligan's Island* "Thurston Howell III" effect that turns people off?

That's going to depend on your audience. You're probably okay if you're selling to a very upscale crowd, but most people will probably not relate to the extreme wealth that a Bentley suggests. Indeed, they may even resent you or figure you're going to overcharge them to pay for your luxurious lifestyle.

Living in Southern California, I'm surrounded by a car culture that demands your automobile reflect your achievement, but within reason. My new Honda made a better, albeit modest, statement about my being good at my craft. My Saturn said I was frugal, but perhaps also a little raggedy around the edges.

So how do you balance appearing both successful and relatable? How do you determine what kind of car to buy or lease? Take a good look at your customers to see what they drive, and then take your cues from them. If you're selling to the BMW crowd, by all means drive a BMW. Your ride will help act as a tool for building that professional image you seek and, in turn, a bridge to your customer base.

A great place to start is with your customer's profile in your business plan. Carefully examine what it is they buy from you, the price points they're willing to pay, the value of their average sale, and where they live. Consider their income and demographics to find a balance point between conservative and flashy that will help customers recognize you as one of their own. If you do it correctly, your customers will admire you and aspire to be like you.

And, since this article is being written in the fall, remember there are three good reasons to remember these lessons—especially at this time of year:

- New car models are being aggressively sold;
- Last year's models still sitting on the dealer's lot are probably a relative bargain; and
- You're plotting your growth strategies for next year and beyond.

Meaning as you're building your New Year's business plan, consider to whom you're selling and what they're driving. If you can create the right formula, it should significantly improve your chances of projecting a relatable image.

This, in turn, will make you more likable and trustworthy. Because, as we all know, people buy from people they know, like, and trust.

FOOD FOR THOUGHT: People buy from people they know, like, and trust.

The Stuffed Sausage in the Gray Dress

Anyone who has visited Las Vegas can't help but be overwhelmed by the experience. Millions of lights make it the brightest physical spot on earth. It boasts 15,000 miles of neon tubing, 300 weddings daily, and consumption of more shellfish every 24 hours than the rest of the country combined.

You get the idea. It's the kind of place where, if you've been there, you don't need an explanation. If you haven't been there, no explanation will truly suffice.

The risks of getting COVID aside, I like going to Vegas to people-watch. Just walk down the street, or into any casino, and you'll see celebrities with parrots on their shoulders, would-be stars, and gawkers and hangers-on of every stripe imaginable.

Yup, this city is both entertaining and educational. You'd think that someone who grew up in New York City would be *way* too cynical for the kitschy experience of Sin City. Yet I'm always fascinated by what I see there. To me, it's kind of like the horror you feel when there's a freeway accident that you can't avert your eyes from.

A big part of going to Vegas is the marketing lessons I take away. Just like at Disneyland, each world has its theme, including Medieval, Egyptian, and Frontierland. Cast members within each "community" have their own flavor of costumes, and the entire Vegas universe is geared toward creating and fulfilling adult fantasies.

Of course, they're ultimately all the same, hawking slightly different approaches to booze, gambling, and entertainment. And they all have the same games, slot machines, and pretty women wearing skimpy outfits.

But here's an interesting bit of trivia about those slot machines. They have them themed for everything from buffalo to Monty Python, but nothing specifically sexually-related. Why? "They're trying to keep the city family-friendly," explains Michael Gottlieb of Mahi Gaming.

A city that creates billions of dollars annually based on nonstop gambling, alcohol, sex, and 83 other kinds of debauchery, and they're trying to keep the city family-friendly by not showing a woman in a bustier on a slot machine.

RIGHT!

About those marketing lessons, though . . . on our last trip I witnessed a woman stuffed into her dress like a sausage into its casing. She was at the craps table, and every time she'd throw the dice she'd shout, "HAPPY BIRTHDAY!"

It didn't help . . . she still lost.

Her personal message ("See my enhanced cleavage?") was unmistakable. Equally obvious was the woman down the gaming floor in green satin hot pants and six-inch spiked heels. And the man in the blond shoulder-length wig and black tube top leaving the lobby of the hotel.

Each used their clothes as packaging to advertise their wares. Arguably, despite the overall smoke-and-mirrors effect, each individual's clothing was the closest one was likely to come to truth in advertising within the confines of the city.

Our own individual packaging also sends a message. Consider, for example, my college intern (a senior) who recently attended a job fair dressed in a suit and tie. Surrounded by a sea of blue jeans and T-shirts, he immediately stood out and earned several highly coveted job interviews.

Coincidence? I think not!

Anyone in sales knows they must sell themselves before they can sell their product or service. And in order to successfully sell yourself, your packaging must match your audience's expectations. Dockers, golf shirt, and loafers in San Diego are appropriate. The same outfit on Wall Street will generate gales of derisive laughter.

So which style will increase your bottom line? One that suits your personality, business, and audience. It should be something you use regularly (like a hat, for instance). Consistently used, those big green shoes or white boutonniere should help you stand out from any given crowd, making you, your company, and your message more memorable.

Remember that whatever you're selling, there are thousands of others who sell the exact same thing. Finding a way to be remembered positively will always give you that edge you seek. Develop both a personal and professional style, and you'll find you're sure to outshine the competition.

Which is why, at the upcoming singles' convention in Vegas, I envision upscale 20-somethings speed-dating, wearing blazers and jeans to broadcast "class" from across the room. Each will be trying to sell themselves. The problem, of course, is that they'll all look alike and still need something to help them be noticed and remembered.

Maybe a big, red rubber nose is in order after all . . .

FOOD FOR THOUGHT: You should *always* be selling yourself! And remember what Mom said: "You only get one chance at making a first impression."

Scott Ginsberg: Marketing Hero!

I've spent a career finding ways for clients in every discipline to stand out from a given crowd. To me, it's obvious that out of sight is out of mind. This makes it critical to be uppermost in a buyer's thoughts if you want that person to think of you when they're finally ready to commit to whatever it is you sell.

Following this thinking, many marketers do something *huge* to grab attention, but then go back to business as usual. Others rely on a steady stream of social media or publicity to remain in the public eye. Still, overwhelmed by the next day's challenges, they'll typically forget to keep their website updated. Or they'll be confronted with the "Can you top this?" syndrome. Unable to outdo themselves, they'll revert to just blending in.

I've always been partial to the professionals who successfully maintain a steady drumbeat of success, rather than the peaks and valleys of intermittent success so many organizations settle for.

These are the marketers who take a holistic approach to their communications efforts. They check all the boxes—with social media, website, sales promotions, events . . . the works. These are the folks universally recognized as successful.

It's unquestionably a challenge to keep such company, and helps explain my consistent use of my hat to help ensure I'm recognized wherever I go.

Obviously, I'm not the only one using personal branding as a marketing tool. Some folks always dress in black; others sport a fresh carnation on their lapel every day.

But Scott Ginsberg is my hero. Starting at age 20, with a desire to be different from everyone else, he started wearing name tags *everywhere*. He found that this caused people to be friendlier and started conversations more easily with countless strangers.

And thus a career was born. "I found treasure where others saw trash," he recalls. "And I vowed to wear a name tag all day, every day, for the rest of my life."

Think of that. Decades of consistently wearing a name tag saying "Hello. My name is Scott." They're on his overcoat, his blazer, and his shirt. He carries spares in his wallet in case the glue wears off.

And yes, if you remove his shirt, he's got a name-tag tattoo. Now *that* is commitment!

Scott leveraged his distinction into a business, training major corporations about approachability. He's built a publishing empire, and been featured in hundreds of media outlets like CNN, *USA Today*, and the *Wall Street Journal*.

His website reports: "Since 1999, Scott Ginsberg has profitably created 50 books, 11 musical albums, 3,000 articles, 600 speeches, 88 training videos, 6 software applications, 3 music films and 1 globally recognized brand."

RIPLEY'S Believe It or Not says he's the world-record holder for wearing name tags.

Google Scott and you'll find he's internationally recognized as "The World's Expert on Name Tags" (which is not as dubious a distinction as one might have previously thought) and "The Authority on Approachability." He's frequently interviewed by various online, print, radio, and TV media for his unique expertise.

Think he ever gets lost in the crowd? *Not on your life!*

Scott's TED Talk is perhaps the most entertaining and informative video I've seen in years. I just invited him to (hopefully) speak at my Rotary Club.

And at every step he asks a simple question: How committed are you to your branding efforts?

It's a worthy discussion to have as you do next year's business planning. If you're just looking to do more of the same, you're sure to get the same kinds of results. And if that works for you, great.

But if you're looking for something different, try looking at the world differently, like Scott Ginsberg does. He's shaken up my thinking, and will probably do the same for you.

After all, as he observes, "It doesn't have to be a name tag; it just has to stick."

════════════════════════

FOOD FOR THOUGHT: Making yourself memorable in little ways may open some big doors for your success.

Five Minutes of Branding. A Lifetime of Love.

I t was a warm August night in 1987 when I set out for Shea Stadium to see the Mets play the Chicago Cubs. I was relatively new to New York City, having moved there after a youthful marriage to my childhood sweetheart fell apart.

So, joined by three friends from around Manhattan, we watched the Mets trounce the Cubs and the crowd was jubilant. This was also the environment on the number 7 subway as I headed home.

11pm on a Friday night in a New York subway car is not when one typically expects to begin a new romance, but the stars had lined up for me that evening. Separated by the crowd from my friends, I found myself 18 inches away from a fellow strap hanger. She, too, was distanced from her traveling companions, and we stood there, eyeing each other.

She was cute, and about my age. I noticed her friendly smile and a face full of freckles, made prominent from her recent vacation on Cape Cod. And, not being particularly shy—and with little at risk beyond possibly getting a smack in the mouth—I asked her a question certain to set me apart from the crowd.

You've probably already noticed that I'm a bit of a character. (The hat should have been the tipoff.) Knowing this, it probably comes as no surprise that my first words to this attractive young woman were "Excuse me, but do you mind if I play connect the dots with your freckles?"

Now truth be told I was *not* trying to pick her up; I genuinely wanted to play connect the dots with her freckles. And, to her credit, she took this comment in the spirit with which it was meant, laughing and responding with a legitimate New York City answer.

Our conversation proceeded as follows (and I swear I am not making up a word of this!):

"Are you an axe murderer?"

"No."

"Well, you weren't sweating when you said that, so I guess it's okay."

Truly the beginning of a New York love story!

And it turned out we lived two blocks apart on the Upper East Side. So when our subway train hit the Grand Central Station stop, her friends headed south and mine headed west, while she and I headed north . . . together.

Exiting at 77th and Lexington, we stopped at a local bar for a beer, staying up until 4:30 talking about anything and everything. Two nights later we went out on a date, and I must have done *something* right because we've been largely inseparable since then.

I tell you this tale not to brag about having found lifelong happiness, but as a reminder that opportunity is around you at all times. Because, though I could have easily taken an attitude of "New Yorkers don't get involved," or just stood there disinterestedly eyeing the crowd, I instead chose to take a chance and marketed myself a bit.

Anyone who's been involved in sales recognizes that asking for the sale risks rejection. But good marketing can frequently soften up even the most hard-boiled audience.

And since we're all always selling ourselves in some way, success demands toughening up and recognizing that the worst that can happen when you ask for the sale is that your prospect will say "No."

Yet, even getting a no means you've potentially learned something (like what didn't work), thus improving your chances for the next sales pitch.

That balmy summer evening, with the breeze blowing through this delightful young woman's hair, I made a choice we all make every day: I took the risk.

In hindsight, analyzing this extensive series of events allows me to now recognize that the subway car was packed with potential competition. Meaning if I didn't make a move to initiate a conversation, the fellow on her other side might have done so first.

The result of my taking this action is obvious. I was honest about who I was, gambled on getting a positive reaction, knocked out the competition, and closed the deal.

The long-term sale took a lot more effort, of course, but constant messaging, presence before my "customer," and an ongoing campaign ensuring she saw the value of maintaining a relationship with me kept the discussion alive. And, as any smart company does with customers to keep them engaged in the process, I romanced her.

We moved in together a year after we met—almost to the day—and we married exactly a year after that. And today—36 years after that fateful subway ride—I am reminded daily of the importance of being a little different, having honest communications, and taking a risk to stand out from the crowd.

It's a lesson I happily share of the value of presenting your uniqueness, regardless of your audience. Because marketing yourself (or your business) just one time more can easily make the difference between long-term success . . . and going home alone.

FOOD FOR THOUGHT: You'll build long-term quality relationships by being honest about who you are and what value you bring to the conversation.

I Need to Borrow $10 Million

Since I was a kid, I've been watching the Macy's parade every Thanksgiving. Between the actual event and movies like *Miracle on 34th Street*, my family and I have spent countless hours with the clowns, marching bands, and Santa Claus, welcoming in the holiday season.

This year it struck me like a thunderbolt: This parade needs a 40-foot-long, 20-foot-high Panama hat flying over the crowd. It's new. It's fresh. It's fun. And it's certain to initiate a *lot* of conversation . . . not to mention opportunities for selling merchandise by street vendors anxious to rip off the concept.

As I see it, the inflatable hat will be walked down Broadway by 50 people, each wearing a blue blazer, blue jeans, and a Panama hat. Marketbuilding.com will be emblazoned on the headband of the balloon and the hats worn by the balloon tenders.

Figuring it's an easy way to expose my consulting firm to the 3.5 million people on the parade route and the 50 million+ television viewers, I contacted Macy's . . . only to be told they do all the selection and design of these balloons in-house.

Naturally they want the usual suspects—SpongeBob, Spiderman, and Charlie Brown—but it can't be coincidental that Ronald McDonald, the Aflac Duck, and the Pillsbury Doughboy come down Broadway in order. Each is a commercial success, and each is instantly recognizable by even the casual viewer.

Further research uncovered the truth: The fun folks at Macy's want characters that have previous proven commercial success. Period. Everyone knows Charlie Brown, Snoopy, and Woodstock, so those decisions are safe, and therefore no-brainers. But using a character that's not as well known? Something amorphous and without a personality, per se, like a hat? That's too risky. What if someone doesn't like it (though who wouldn't like a Panama hat?)?

What I didn't know was that first-time balloons cost $190,000+ for construction and admission into the parade. In year two, I'd pay Macy's about $90,000 to throw my hat into the ring, as it were.

That works out to be $1,055 per minute for the three-hour parade during year one, and $500 per minute during year two. And since those figures are a bit dated, and given the global helium shortage, the costs of getting a balloon into the parade has probably seen some inflation (*rimshot*).

So I figure slipping my hat into the procession should just be a matter of greasing the right palms. My guess is $10 million ought to cover it all, including fitting all 50 volunteers with costumes and filling my oversized chapeau on Wednesday night with the equivalent of 20,000 helium balloons.

Yet, despite the huge increases in California real estate values, I can't seem to borrow the $10 million against my Carlsbad condo, so I need a little help. I'm thinking a Kickstarter campaign may be in order, though I'm open to other ideas as well. Maybe selling sponsorships with stickers or neon lights on the side of the balloon for all the world to see.

Or maybe I'll have more luck persuading the folks at Macy's to run a sweepstakes where the winner gets to design their own balloon. Kind of like Hudson Rowan's I VOTED sticker, in which a teenager in upstate New York won a contest to bring his artwork significant visibility … only *much* bigger.

To my mind, sliding the hat between Mr. Kool-Aid and Mickey Mouse makes perfect sense. We'll all just sort of glide down Broadway, minding our own business, and make millions of people aware of our existence.

Should be a simple proposition, right?

And on the chance Macy's is determined to hold the line at 16 balloons, I'm drafting a design so the Energizer Bunny can wear my hat instead. That'll at least introduce the concept, and the hat can go solo next year.

Unless Kermit the Frog wants to wear it, of course. I'm easy.

Hey, let's face a fact: The Macy's Thanksgiving parade has become one giant shilling fest. Like the commercials on the Super Bowl, competition is limited and the audience is huge. Ignoring it as a marketing tool would be foolish.

So why shouldn't I sponsor a balloon? The cost per thousand viewers is equivalent to a large email campaign, and I'm sure to stand out from the crowd. Well, over it, anyway.

And let me close with this special offer: For a limited time, if you lend me the money for this venture before February 1, you can even ride on the float with me right behind the balloon.

How's *that* for a deal?

––––––––––––––––––––––––––

FOOD FOR THOUGHT: Thinking a little differently has the potential to help you expand your audience for about the same cost as doing the same old, same old.

Marketing the Dread Pirate Roberts

R ecently I watched the movie *The Princess Bride* for the 35th time. This amusing romp always brightens my mood. While not to everyone's taste, it's an excellent distraction from the day's headlines.

For those unfamiliar with this classic 1987 film, it's a tale of a grandfather reading a book to his sick and skeptical grandson. The grandson allows the reading because it includes fencing, fighting, torture, revenge, giants, monsters, chases, escapes, true love, and miracles.

Yet, as the movie's tagline says, it's also a story of a man and a woman who lived happily ever after...even though the courtship almost killed them.

Having watched this foolishness so many times, I typically split my attention between playing Wordle and the action on screen. Yet there, buried deep within the dialogue, I accidentally uncovered the value of branding.

Now admittedly, I had expected to find fencing, fighting, etc.,...but *not* lessons about marketing.

However, the lightbulb went on over my head when Westley (the hero) describes how he acquired the title "Dread Pirate Roberts" from a line of charlatans, each of whom has previously benefited from a reputation he hadn't earned.

The Dread Pirate Roberts, of course, was the most feared pirate on the local seas, and just the very mention of his name was enough to make strong men quake in their boots.

"The man I inherited it from is not the real Dread Pirate Roberts either," Westley explains. "The real Roberts has been retired fifteen years and living like a king in Patagonia."

He then clarifies to the heroine (Buttercup) that Dread Pirate Roberts is a title more than a person. "Pirates and sailors need to fear their captain, and nothing strikes fear into the hearts of men like the name of the Dread Pirate Roberts!"

His conclusion: "Nobody would ever surrender to the Dread Pirate Westley."

There it was! The power of branding, all boiled down to a few words. Of course, I'd heard this snippet of dialogue dozens of times but hadn't previously made the connection. The Dread Pirate Roberts had successfully branded himself as so fearsome that anyone sporting that name would be feared. But the same guy, calling himself the Dread Pirate Westley (and no matter how mean-spirited) would have to start from scratch in building his reputation.

INCONCEIVABLE!

I've been in the marketing trenches since 1981. In that time I've met countless business owners who wonder why they need to devote attention to their marketing. An attitude of "I sell quality, and people will flock to me," isn't uncommon.

These entrepreneurs see marketing communications as something to be tolerated, not nurtured. An expense, rather than an investment.

And they're invariably shocked when rapid success eludes them . . . largely because they haven't thought through the entire process.

They obviously haven't seen *The Princess Bride*!

Here's the thing: regardless of what you sell, it's important to remember that your company's brand includes its name, logo, reputation, products, services, people, pricing, and a dozen little things bringing the business to life.

But your business's success doesn't just happen. There's no magic drawer containing an effective communications strategy. No wizard will deliver to you an award-winning website, first position on Google, or a video that goes viral . . . while you're off storming the castle.

In fact, every marketing success takes a lot of intensive planning, hard work, and extensive investment. And nothing in marketing happens by accident.

That's why you must outmaneuver the competition, and not be afraid to build on someone else's success.

True, there will be setbacks along the way, and success isn't guaranteed. But hard work, dedication, good quality, fair pricing, a solid communications strategy, and intelligent messaging can be combined to help *you* live happily ever after.

And, if you do it right, it won't kill you.

―――――――――――――

FOOD FOR THOUGHT: Hard work, dedication, good quality, fair pricing, a solid communications strategy, and intelligent messaging can be combined to help *you* live happily ever after.

Laughing at My Blue Jeans

One of the nice things about being a marketing consultant is you can wriggle your way into conversations with some *very* interesting people.

And I've always been told two things: Clothes make the man, and you can only get one chance to make a first impression.

I moved to San Diego in 2002 with these two philosophies firmly in mind. And shortly after I hit town, I was able to meet with Costco's regional VP to discuss some off-the-wall—but potentially lucrative—ideas for the company.

Reasoning he's a vice president of a multinational corporation, I put on a suit and shined my shoes. After all, I was presenting myself as the former principal of a New York ad agency, and figured I should dress the part.

So imagine my surprise to see this fellow at his desk wearing ratty jeans, a golf shirt, and threadbare sneakers. Hanging from the bare white walls was a nail and some picture wire.

That's when something in my brain broke, as there was an obvious disconnect between what I'd been expecting and what reality had delivered.

The gentleman politely spent 15 minutes listening to my pitch before walking me out of his inner sanctum. I'd accomplished nothing, and I was disappointed as my fantasies of wealth evaporated in the afternoon sun.

Crestfallen at my failure, I pestered him mercilessly for the next several weeks until he finally agreed to have another conversation with me.

This time I took no chances. It was apparent to even the most casual observer that the client's style was more relaxed than mine, and in true Darwinian fashion, I'd need to adapt if I wanted to survive.

Which is why, when I appeared at his door wearing sandals, jeans, golf shirt, sunglasses, and hat, he smiled and said (and I'm *not* making this up!), "Now you've got it. *Now* we can talk business."

He added, "I've had guys come here eight, ten times and they just never figure it out." We then spent an hour spitballing concepts.

Furthermore, he liked my ideas so much that we developed prototypes that went to headquarters before being shot down.

And though things never proceeded beyond these initial stages, I learned a great deal that day about building client relationships.

It's important to remember that you're always selling yourself to clients, and that means personality, grooming, clothing, and style. It's why I always try to smell nice, speak well, appear sober, and dress appropriately for any given occasion.

And it's why, as you're looking to increase your own market prominence, it's important to consider the audience to whom you're selling and to help them feel comfortable around you.

Mirroring the way a prospective client dresses can be a big first step toward building that bridge. After all, people do business with those they know, like, and trust. If someone thinks you're like them, they're more likely to want to trust you.

This applies to the organizations you belong to, where you live, how you speak, and (of course) what you wear.

Of course, dressing for success depends on both the individual and that person's audience. My appearing in a suit that first day at a jeans-riddled organization broadcast a message of stiffness. Had I more carefully considered Costco's casual culture, I'd have realized that my wearing jeans and a blazer would have probably made more sense.

But hailing from New York City, I defaulted to my Big Apple wardrobe. Indeed, in my native New York the jeans and blazer would have been scoffed at, with the suit and tie de rigueur.

Thus, it became a judgment call, and fortunately, I was able to recover from my mistake.

Admittedly, I'm always sporting the hat, regardless of whatever else I'm wearing. That's my brand, and an easy hook for strangers trying to spot me in a crowd. As you now know, I've worn it so consistently that many don't recognize me without it.

Plus, whether I'm dressed up or down, the hat announces I'm creative. Which probably explains why so many people give me a free pass on the hat, chalking it up to personal style. And that generosity encourages them to focus even more on the rest of my wardrobe, as that completes the picture and announces who I *really* am.

As you seek your next opportunity, consider how your audience dresses, and try to find ways to appear like them without being too obsequious. You might be surprised at how effective it can be as a selling tool.

FOOD FOR THOUGHT: You're always selling yourself to clients, and that means personality, grooming, clothing, and style.

Have You Tried Wearing Moose Antlers?

A ttend any chamber of commerce event and you're sure to encounter eight realtors, four mortgage brokers, and six bankers. Each will earnestly tell you they offer great service and wonderful rates. Each wants your business.

And you're sure to forget all of them before you get back to your car.

Because odds are good that every one of these professionals is going to dress like the others. Sure, there will be different color suits or ties. They'll probably also comb their hair in different ways.

But nothing is going to make any of them stand out enough to stick in your mind for the short-term. And unless you give them your contact information, you may never hear from them again, nor recognize them at the next chamber meeting.

Furthermore, unless there's something really memorable about you, they probably won't recognize you the next time, either.

What everyone in this scenario lacks is some type of personal branding—an effort to find someone's uniqueness, build a reputation on the things they want to be known for, and create a visual that conveys a message that can ultimately be monetized in some way.

A good example of personal branding might be Donald Trump. Like him or hate him, you know who he is because he's a master at keeping a consistent image in front of you at all times.

Let's look at it from another angle: When you see McDonald's golden arches, the odds are excellent you'll have an emotional response (good or bad) associated with the company. Even without seeing the name, the image alone can make you feel warm and fuzzy, angry, etc.

Obviously, you instantly recognize those arches because the company has invested tremendous resources to remind you who they belong to and to drive you in to do business with them.

Personal branding is the individual's equivalent of those arches, creating a consistent impression that allows you to achieve both your personal and professional goals.

As Amazon CEO Jeff Bezos once said, "Your brand is what people say about you when you're not in the room." Obviously, you want to make sure they're saying something good.

⸻

Now consider the following situation that happened in Carlsbad, California, a coastal community just north of San Diego.

There's a woman I know there who is blonde, possesses a nice figure, and has a brilliant smile.

She once asked for help on her personal branding efforts. "I see myself sporting a low-cut white blouse and my smile," she said.

Admittedly, my reaction wasn't what she hoped for. I found myself hard-pressed to see any one smiling blonde in a low-cut blouse being different from a thousand other women similarly attired . . . especially in Southern California.

The need to make her stand out from the crowd forced us to come up with something else—something she could commit to, day and night, inside and out.

And, like me with my hat, she had to choose something she was comfortable with.

Having the right personal branding can be a powerful advantage in today's world. An attractive blonde will typically not be noticed amongst the competition just for being an attractive blonde. Yet, put a red hibiscus flower in her hair and she'll stand a much better chance of being recognized more often . . . especially if she's wearing that flower every time you see her.

Because it's easy to get lost in any crowd, and many people go to great lengths to avoid being forgotten. This need to be noticed is what leads many folks to get tattoos, shave odd designs into their hair, or wear oversized eyeglasses with rhinestones.

Sometimes it even works!

In my case, Renaissance Executive Forums coach Jim Tenuto accurately observed, "Without his hat, Rob Weinberg would be just another middle-aged Rancho Bernardo dude."

Naturally, my blonde friend isn't the only one I've encountered with personal branding challenges. In fact, one might argue that every one of us has to deal with the same issue.

And with America's population now over 335 million, there's an increasing need to distinguish yourself, both in personal and professional settings.

However, by building on your personal style, you can make yourself stand out a bit . . . regardless of your business.

You may be comfortable always carrying an umbrella or walking stick, or chronically wearing red. You could be the guy wearing a lime-green fedora with a peacock feather sticking out.

Even sporting a hat resembling moose antlers could work, though I'd suggest against it if you're in fields involving finance, law, or similar areas demanding a more somber attitude.

However, whatever style you choose to implement for yourself, you *must* commit to it long-term. Because if you're like those companies that change business strategies every three months, you're only going to confuse people.

Select an image for yourself that can work for you long-term and then, like your company's logo and tagline, brand it into the minds of customers, prospects, and the community at-large.

There's a great deal to be said for good, consistent personal branding, as it can significantly improve your chances of being remembered. Because, as my blonde friend discovered, merely saying "I'm better than or different from the competition," but not giving customers a simple way to remember you, is a virtual guarantee that you'll be forgotten within moments of leaving the room.

FOOD FOR THOUGHT: Just looking like everyone else is a guarantee you'll be forgotten.

Can This Issue Be Solved By the Right . . . or the Left?

For the past several decades, it's become increasingly obvious that right versus left is a problem threatening to overthrow our system of doing business as usual.

No, I'm not referring to Republican vs. Democrat, but rather a *much* bigger question: On which lapel should you wear your name badge?

The overwhelming importance of this issue struck me when I attended a reception last night. There I noticed almost everyone in the room had their name badge on the left side of their jackets or blouses. There were an even half-dozen of us with our badges on the right side (out of a crowd of 150 or so). The six of us all had a background in sales or marketing.

So while Miss Manners might tell you there's no difference on which side one wears a name badge, I believe there is an advantage to wearing the badge on the right side for those wishing to communicate a point quickly and effectively.

Let's start with some background on shaking hands. Folklore tells us that an ancient villager automatically withdrew his dagger when meeting a stranger. Once persuaded the situation wasn't dangerous, the weapon would be sheathed and the right hand—the weapon hand—would be extended empty as a token of goodwill.

No, I'm *not* making this stuff up!

Now add to this historical footnote the fact that roughly 90 percent of people are right-handed. Furthermore, in the US we put our right hand over our heart when saying the Pledge of Allegiance. It's a short leap from these facts to slapping a label over the heart with the right hand. If you don't believe me, ask Scott Ginsberg (Personal Branding article 3).

Within easy reach of the right hand also happens to be where most men's shirt pockets are located, which is probably just an odd coincidence.

Now examine the handshake itself. Because of the overwhelming preponderance of right-handed people, you're typically expected to extend your right hand, look at the hand you're shaking, then look at the face of the person you're meeting. Your eyeball instinctively follows past the hand, flows up the arm, turns right at the shoulder, and settles on the face seeking a smile.

If the person you're meeting has a name badge on the left lapel, you'll easily find the face but have to search to figure out who the heck you're addressing.

However, had that same person worn the name badge on the right lapel, your introduction would have gone a bit smoother. You'd have clasped their hand, followed the line of the arm, stopped momentarily at the name badge to cue your brain and/or refresh your memory, gone up to the shoulder, and settled on the face. All in less time than it took you to read this paragraph.

This almost makes sense, doesn't it? We want to do business with those we know, like, and trust. We're more likely to like and trust those who make us feel comfortable. One easy way to make a stranger feel comfortable is to help them know your name. And the easiest, most subtle way to do that at a meeting is by making it easier to find your name badge.

Of course, there's nothing saying you'll make more money, get that cutie in the corner to have a drink with you, or eliminate your halitosis by wearing your name badge on your right lapel. Indeed, there's no guarantee of success from doing any of the things I suggest in my columns. (My lawyer made me write that. Okay, Jim? *Now* will you stop pestering me?) But when you consider:

- how hard it is to stand out of a given crowd,
- how easy it is to make people more comfortable,
- how you can use this approach to open a conversation, and
- how few people wear their name badges on the right side,

this business hack actually simplifies your business dealings a bit.

You can even draw more attention to your identity by wearing a pin from a group you belong to (Rotary, American Legion, fraternity, etc.) on your lapel above the badge.

As a marketer, I'm a big believer in test-marketing. You find a message that works, then try to improve it. So why not use this as a marketing test? Assuming you've always worn your name badge on the left side, try wearing it on the right for the next five events you attend. Tell people what you're doing and why. See how they respond.

If, after the test is over, it appears I'm full of beans (yeah—like *that* could ever happen, right?), you can always revert to your old ways. I expect you'll get good results, though, and anticipate you'll permanently wear your badge on the right side from now on.

═══════════════════════════════

FOOD FOR THOUGHT: Wearing your name badge on the right side makes it easier to initiate a business conversation.

There's a Little Less Me Out There Today

This past January 1 I did the one thing you're never supposed to do as the holidays are ending: I stepped on the scale.

Oh, the pain. Ach, the anguish! Oy, the *torture*!

Frankly, I don't know *what* I was thinking. I wasn't hungover or otherwise impaired, and I'm usually smart enough to avoid such self-inflicted cruelty.

Yet here I was in my underwear, assessing the damage from the previous six weeks . . . and it wasn't pretty. I was reminded of that country song, "I Don't Look Good Naked Anymore."

But I digress. On January 1 I weighed in at my heaviest ever. I started getting agitated, until I remembered the words of my old boss Martina. When I first got started in the business world, she advised me, "A heart attack or a tax audit is a crisis. Everything else in life is a situation you just have to deal with."

Wise words indeed. So I decided to deal with this situation, and over the next several days I developed a strategy for losing 20 pounds by year end.

I'm not a big believer in New Year's resolutions. So many people that I know make them, then break them within weeks. The way I figure it, if I'm going to break a promise I made to myself, I don't need the formality of a public statement to enshrine the event.

Still, I wanted to look svelte. My role models were the countless beautiful people I'd seen in advertising, movies, and television shows. My doctor also said it would help my health to knock off a few pounds.

Of course, the fact that it was cheaper to lose the weight than to buy a new wardrobe was also a good incentive.

So I worked hard all year, approaching this as if it were a business challenge that needed to be resolved. I became aware of every morsel I put into my mouth, even when (or especially when) I cheated.

I ate less junk (cookies, chips) and replaced much of the wine I'd been drinking with water. And I walked the dog a lot more.

Which is why I'm pleased to be able to announce I've met my goal slightly ahead of schedule. It's Thanksgiving again, and my clothes are fitting better. True, my dietary tastes haven't really changed, but for the moment my days of endless piles of French fries and glasses of beer are behind me.

Developing and implementing a workable plan—what a concept! By approaching this challenge with a strategy, tactics, goals, milestones, and dedication, I succeeded.

Yes, by all means go ahead and pop that bottle of champagne . . . though you'll excuse me if I only have a sip or two.

There's also been an interesting side effect. Trim or chunky, I've noticed how I only seem to come into focus to friends and strangers alike when I'm wearing my hat. I attribute it to a steady diet of writing, public speaking, newsletters, social media, and references from satisfied clientele.

Those beautiful people I used to envy also have a plan for being attractive and noticeable in public. The Brad Pitts of the world are promoted using publicity, social media, blockbuster advertising, the occasional phony marriage, and lots of packaging using makeup, lighting, and their secret weapon: Photoshop.

In other words . . . they're really no different from the rest of us.

And when they get grossly overweight they lose some of the luster they've struggled so hard to gain.

These musings might give you something to consider as the calendar turns again, as they suggest a few potential avenues toward your business success in the coming 12 months:

1. Envision realistic goals, then work hard to make them happen.

2. Recognize how we're manipulated by the media around us.

3. Regardless of what you do or sell, understand that there's never any success without good marketing.

As the New Year bears down upon us once more, you've undoubtedly got your business plan in place and have given serious thought to what makes your organization different from the competition. You know your objectives, have a budget and milestones, and understand the importance of separating the marketing and sales components.

What you may have forgotten, though, is how quality messaging, consistently presented, will make you unforgettable. The other guy shouldn't be envied, because the key to success lies within each of us.

FOOD FOR THOUGHT: A heart attack or a tax audit is a crisis. Everything else in life is a situation you just have to deal with.

The Dentist without Teeth

===

You've heard me say before how my mother always told me you get one shot at a first impression. It helps explain why I shine my shoes, don't wear wrinkled shirts, and always try to smell nice. After all, you never know who you're going to be introduced to when you go out, right?

So imagine my surprise when I noticed my dentist missing a tooth.

I've been friends with this fellow for over 20 years, know he does good work, and we just laughed about it. Seemed he'd had an accident, and hadn't yet had time to go to *his* dentist to get the problem fixed.

I fully anticipate a lot of good-natured ribbing over this incident in the years to come.

From there, my attention turned to this morning's sales call, with me the prospective client. This salesperson and I talked for 10 minutes about a high-ticket item, and his unwillingness or inability to look me in the eye troubled me. For the moment, I've decided not to do business with him.

In each of these instances, a service provider had a customer before him. Unlike packaged goods, which typically tend to be marketed as commodity items, service providers have an opportunity to quickly stand out and show what additional value they bring to a given conversation.

Of course, this all assumes they're making a good impression; something neither of these guys were doing. And it's a lesson we can all benefit from.

People buy from those they know, like, and trust. Someone who is unwilling to look me in the eye suggests he's shifty and trying to pick my pocket. I'm unable to readily trust him.

A dentist with a gap tooth appears incompetent.

Try it another way . . . would you be likely to buy a Mercedes-Benz from a guy who drives a beaten-up pickup truck and dresses in coveralls without a shirt? It's doubtful, as his personal presentation is completely off-brand.

Mind you, I've been known to drive beaten-up vehicles myself, and sloppy clothes and I are not strangers.

However, selling effectively means selling yourself. This necessitates packaging yourself to appear in the same category as what you're selling. Selling a Rolls-Royce? Dressing impeccably is called for. Marketing surfboards? Grab that Hawaiian shirt.

You get the idea . . . it's all about context and packaging.

As for the guy who couldn't look me in the eye, it's true that he might have been nervous or distracted, and I'm being judgmental. For all I knew, it was his first day on the job. I know I was nervous on *my* first day in sales, when my first prospective client actually gave me two orders: "Get out!" and "Stay out!"

Yet, as the customer I am entitled to certain expectations, and a feeling of trust with someone to whom I'm going to hand over my money is one of them. This man's failure to look me square in the eye made me suspicious. Of course in time he may still earn my trust—assuming he makes the effort to stay in touch and continue selling to me—but for the moment I'm going to move forward with him cautiously.

As a youth I learned we're all in sales to a certain extent. Kids need to sell the urgency of getting a bigger allowance, students want better grades from the teacher, and singles desire to convince that hot new neighbor to go out for drinks. Each requires the art of persuasion, eventually (and hopefully) selling someone to accept your point of view. Recognizing this, and regardless of the overall objective of your next conversation, perhaps we can all gather something of value from today's events.

As you prepare for your next meeting, consider whether you're:

- Looking your sales prospect in the eye. If that makes you uncomfortable, look at the bridge of the nose instead.
- Looking your best, including dressing similarly to your customer.
- Presenting your most professional image, and one that is appropriate to whatever you're selling.

This last point could mean a realtor driving a fancy car to indicate sales success. And a landscaper better have a *really* nice garden to show off at their own home.

But a personal trainer who's not really fit may know their stuff, but will have trouble selling themselves well. And a writer who says "um" and "like" every third word . . . well, let's just say there's a credibility issue there.

Which brings us full circle back to my dentist, whom I advised to fix his image problem lest it negatively impact his bottom line.

Because unless he's able to provide visible proof of the quality of his work, claims that he'll improve your smile will appear toothless.

Bah dum dum!

FOOD FOR THOUGHT: If you don't make a good presentation for yourself with what you do professionally, don't expect anyone else to hire you.

Marketing Can Be a Hairy Business

My editor once asked how I got my ideas for these columns, and the answer was surprisingly simple: I pay attention to the world around me. Apropos of absolutely nothing is this interesting example.

One of the things I've noticed over the years is how most politicians are clean-shaven. From Dwight Eisenhower to Ronald Reagan, Harry Truman to Barack Obama, and everyone in between, there's nary a whisker in sight.

The reason? Potential voters need to feel comfortable before they will want to support a candidate. And as a rule, people generally don't feel comfortable buying things from men with beards or mustaches.

There are exceptions, of course. Pennsylvania senator John Fetterman is a good example.

But Mr. Fetterman aside, consider the subtle message the overwhelming majority typically takes away from a beard and its wearer. Because the message voters perceive about candidates for office are very similar to the message prospective customers probably take away about you in business if you have facial hair.

Especially if you have it when you first meet them, as that's the thing that will stick in their minds as a distinguishing feature.

Now some may say a marketing column is no place to discuss facial hair. However, regular readers of my columns know I believe you sell yourself rather than selling any particular product or service.

So if you have a beard and/or mustache and don't close as many deals as you'd like to, see if any of these subliminal reactions sound familiar to you:

- "You're professorial." Beards are oftentimes the province of college professors, computer engineers, and serious research types. While that suggests that you're smart, you're probably

not going to be seen as having the salesperson personality needed to educate and persuade me to buy whatever you're selling.

- "You're a creative type." The marketing industry relies on combining both sides of the brain to be successful, and right-brained
types are generally the guys wearing beards. In my experience,
though, odds are better that those who do wear beards will not
be as adept at finessing social situations or addressing short-
term client needs as their clean-shaven counterparts on the
account management side of the business.

- "You're hiding something." That beard gives you a wall to
hide behind, making you appear shifty and/or untrustworthy. If
you're not sneaky, then why won't you let me see your face?

- "You're unkempt." In a society as obsessed with cleanliness
as ours claims to be, beards may be hiding bits of yesterday's
lunch that are still on your person.

As a youth I remember my father guiding me away from wearing
facial hair if I wanted to be successful in business. True, I once grew a
mustache, but it looked like a caterpillar fell asleep on my upper lip and
did absolutely *nothing* to help move either my career or my social life
forward.

Somewhere around here I have a photo of me from those days, but
it's *not* a pretty sight! Trust me on this one.

Furthermore, given that I'm hardly what one would call hirsute, persuading me to lose the mustache wasn't a particularly tough sell for my
dad. Still, I was intrigued by men with walrus mustaches and the like. I
thought guys who used mustache wax were really cool, and have always
admired the ability to shave, then show up sporting a full beard about 20
minutes later.

Still, from a marketing perspective what kinds of people first jump
into your mind when you think of men with facial hair?

- Adolph Hitler
- Charlie Chaplin
- Saddam Hussein
- Snidely Whiplash

All of them are creeps or clowns. None are people you'd want handling your next real estate transaction, eh?

And the politicians? For many people, Fidel Castro comes to mind ...despite him being dead since 2016.

Now consider this: Of our 46 presidents (at this writing), only 5 had beards, 5 had mustaches (counting Cleveland's two terms), and 2 had sideburns, giving us 74 percent that were clean-faced. In fact, beards in American politics haven't been in vogue pretty much since the days of Benjamin Harrison (ca. 1893). Mustaches went out with the Taft administration in 1912.

These guys obviously know something.

Which suggests it shouldn't be a big leap to see that the most successful salespeople are also clean-shaven. People like Warren Buffett, Jeff Bezos, and Bill Gates are all at the top of my list.

Of course, none of this should suggest that having a beard or a mustache makes you a bad person. Even my old friend Susie in Oshkosh, Wisconsin, who has a rather pronounced mustache, has been able to find love.

However, it does suggest that someone interested in marketing themself—which is key to being able to sell any other message—will probably improve the odds by doing it sans facial hair.

FOOD FOR THOUGHT: Many would-be customers think a salesperson with facial hair is shifty or untrustworthy. Being clean-shaven invariably improves your chances of making the sale.

I'm Judgmental; You Got a Problem with That?

As the owner of a small business, I typically bring in college interns for extra hands at low cost.

Having participated in several internships myself during my college career, I recognize the benefits on all sides. The student gets solid, practical experience that can be leveraged after graduation with prospective employers. Employers have someone lower on the totem pole that they can push entry-level work toward (maximizing their more senior staff's talents). And schools arranging these relationships can offer something extra of value.

Which is why my annual hunt for the right personality and skill set is such an interesting experiment. My task becomes finding someone with good research and writing abilities who can make deadlines, deliver quality results, be presentable to clients, and laugh at my jokes.

That final item, by the way, is not always an easy job. I'm a big believer in dad jokes like "A mushroom walks into a bar. The bartender says 'Hey, get out of here; we don't serve your kind' and the mushroom says (wait for it) 'Why not? I'm a fun guy.'"

Bah dum dum! I'm here until Thursday, folks. Try the vegetable scramble, and don't forget to tip your server.

To find the right person to fill these internships, I've tried connecting through joinhandshake.com, family friends, and college professor referrals. Regardless of my resources, though, it's always a challenge. Being inexperienced, students can be forgiven for not recognizing they're interviewing for a job, have competition, and must present their best face.

Along the way I've gotten some real gems. However you interpret that word is probably how I meant it.

This knowledge gap probably also explains why I've interviewed college women with bare midriffs and pierced navels and men with huge holes in their earlobes. For them it's just expressing who they are, and their attire is of no concern if they're tucked in a back room, doing all their communications on the phone or via email, or dealing with customers who are similarly dressed.

But I'm a communications professional who meets clients either face-to-face or via Zoom, and I require someone on my team who can make a quality representation when meeting with clients in their thirties . . . and in their seventies. And, with no offense intended toward anyone, let's be realistic for a moment—someone who spent years running a multinational corporation typically isn't going to take a 21-year-old with a visibly pierced navel very seriously.

Few of these kids get hired for this type of position, and my attitude unquestionably limits my pool of prospects.

But what if your prospective intern knows how to dress the part, but doesn't speak well?

Phonetics professor Henry Higgins (*Pygmalion*) noted that in America they hadn't used English for years. In fact, ESL (English as a Second Language) classes can help the individual whose primary language isn't English. But someone who's native born but doesn't take the time to learn the language, or isn't concerned with proper grammar, accurate spelling, and ways to speak properly . . . well, that's another story.

For example, there's a college senior whom I recently considered for my internship program. He appeared right for the job, but every third word of his was "like." I found myself unable to listen to him, and decided against hiring him.

The truth is I couldn't wait to stop listening to him.

It feels like I'm increasingly surrounded by people saying "like." It's a verbal tic, replacing "um" and "er" in the vernacular. I find it annoying, and have been known to ask these individuals to say the exact same sentence without using the word "like." If they can't, I quickly tune them out, and know our future interactions will be limited.

Dr. Alan Brownlie, an English professor at Anne Arundel Community College in Baltimore, likens this tic to a hamster running on a wheel, stopping periodically to catch his breath. "The 'likes,' 'ums,' and 'ers' are that person stopping to catch his breath while searching for the next word," he says.

It's beyond me why there can't just be a moment of silence while that person searches for the proper word to use in a sentence, but this is the apparent reality I'm working with.

My millennial daughter says I'm too judgmental, and maybe she's right. However, I'm a communications professional who works hard to say the same thing in different ways. I keep a thesaurus on my desk, recognizing there are words that just won't appear in my online searches. And finding the right word for the right situation can oftentimes be the critical difference between success and failure.

This means working with someone who only seems to say different things the same way is out of the question.

Said Professor Higgins, "The majesty and grandeur of the English language is the greatest possession we have." He referred to its "extraordinary, imaginative, and musical mixtures of sounds."

I agree.

I know . . . this desire for linguistic perfection is probably seen by many as quaint, and potentially puts me into the category of old fogey. Still, it depresses me that so many people have either ignored or forgotten the joys of using language well. And while I appreciate the word "like," too much of anything is unpleasant.

Bottom line: Business owners concerned with their public image should think hard before hiring someone who doesn't represent them well in every way. The job market can be fickle, even in the best of times. Which means an inability to communicate well makes selling yourself to potential employers critical for your own success.

FOOD FOR THOUGHT: Job seekers are advised to dress nicely, have a professional-looking resume, and be prompt for any meetings. For me, add speaking well to the list.

Business Branding

Must You Be So Strict?

=====================================

Anyone looking to improve their company's image should remember two words: branding consistency.

From Amazon to Xerox, the most successful businesses have consistent branding that consumers instantly recognize. Their respective images are driven home repeatedly using publicity, direct mail, print advertising, television, invoice stuffers, internet banner ads, and a *ton* of social media.

"But Coke uses different themes for their advertising," I hear you cry. True enough. Yet whether they're showing kids at the beach or an animated polar bear, the company's umbrella "look" for their marketing materials informs you at every turn that it's coming from the same source. They always use the same font, colors, logo, and tagline to impart a unified impression, and their steady drumbeat enables them to integrate into our daily lives.

Your company's image speaks volumes about you, your product, and your service. Adhering to a consistent branding image is important for every business, oftentimes making the difference in whether or not your clientele remembers you in the future. Like Coke, be sure to always use the same:

- **FONT.** Choose one that suits your style—high tech, adventurous, fun, etc. A shoe manufacturer might benefit from using a typeface where the letters all look like shoes.
- **COLORS.** Select your company colors wisely, as each color carries certain meanings and generates certain reactions. One product's color convinces us it tastes fresher than the same product with a different color.
- **LOGO.** This instantly allows customers to identify your company, products, and services, giving them an emotional reaction to the experience they anticipate from you.

- **TAGLINE**. In under 10 words, encapsulate the message you want customers to take away about your organization.

Once you've committed to these four items, start slapping them (and your URL) onto everything: business cards, operations manuals, trade show booths, brochures . . . the works. Over time, customers will see the logo and remember the message . . . and you.

Then, by directing people to your website, they'll learn more about your products, services, history, philosophy, and how to buy from you.

A steady corporate image is critical to being seen as a serious player. Consider the American Automobile Association, which demands that anything created for them must use "AAA Red." They have a three-inch thick binder full of rules and regulations for their designers and printers to follow. Address lines must be so many centimeters from the edge of the paper, and logos must be just so large for certain sizes of paper.

To ensure the same red is used by all vendors, AAA specifies its color from the Pantone Matching System, also known as PMS. PMS is a system established to provide continuity between designers and printers, dictating how many parts cyan (a color between green and blue), yellow, magenta (purplish-red), and black ink are needed to reproduce a color perfectly every time.

Which is why, if you say "PMS 192" to any graphic designer or printer, they'll all show you the same shade of red. When combining their rules with the color system, AAA guarantees a consistent company look, whether the brochure is produced in New York or Los Angeles. Suppliers are expected to adhere to these rules *without exception*!

Furthermore, someone in the marketing department must approve all communications materials before they're produced to ensure such consistency. It's why you'll never see a AAA logo in green.

You should also have someone on your management team overseeing the process of developing the logo, tagline, company colors, and all marketing materials. This person will be your "logo police" and be tasked with shepherding your communications materials through the development and internal approval process.

Trust me, all this work is worth it. Because there's nothing so unprofessional as a rack of sales flyers, each printed in a different shade of blue. Or a display of business cards where half have one design and half another.

Bottom line: Whether you're a start-up or a mature company, having customized designs or working with prepackaged templates, keep your style consistent across all your marketing materials. You'll be amazed at how much more professional it makes you look.

And yes . . . people *will* notice.

—————————————————

FOOD FOR THOUGHT: There is *no* downside to having a consistent company image throughout your marketing materials. It's something that people who are serious about their business can't afford to ignore.

You've Never Made a Mistake?

It seems like only yesterday that IHOP—the International House of Pancakes—made a big announcement: They were changing their name to IHOb, standing for International House of Burgers. This exercise (in June 2018) was all to introduce a new item (a burger) on their menu.

This change got lots of online chatter and the restaurants changed their signs for a month before reverting to the original company moniker. Yet, though lots of folks were talking about the company, their sales didn't increase much at all.

IHOP wasn't the only major corporation to screw around with their branding. For 79 days in 1985, Coca-Cola yanked its traditional formula to make way for "New Coke." Coke had been using the same closely guarded secret combination of ingredients for a century, and abruptly announced a mixture that would be bolder, rounder, and more harmonious tasting.

It was also markedly sweeter, in an effort to counter the more sugary appeal of Pepsi, which was encroaching on Coke's market share.

Eight thousand customers a day called to complain as their drink of choice was no longer available . . . leading in short order to the rejuvenation of "Old Coke." The company was left with egg on their face, desperately trying to spin the story as best they could.

Then there was the 2010 Gap logo debacle, where Gap attempted to transition their image from classic, American design to modern, sexy, and cool. The only problem? Consumers immediately rejected the new logo . . . and six days later Gap was back to the traditional look.

Pepsi. Bloomingdale's. American Airlines. Audi. The list of companies that have had big-time marketing errors is both impressive and endless. Many have resulted in millions of dollars in losses, and all have been public relations disasters.

Some of them were driven by financial desperation, others by a failed attempt at using humor. All of them seem to have one thing in common:

not talking with enough customers in advance to see how people unconnected with the company would react.

Yup, even Coke test-marketing their new formula to 200,000 consumers just wasn't enough to foresee the tsunami of protest. Or perhaps they just didn't ask the right questions.

Then there was the 2017 Dove Facebook video of three women of different ethnicities, each removing a T-shirt to reveal the next woman. The intention was to celebrate diversity and convey that its body wash is for every woman.

However, it was perceived as a Black woman transforming into a White woman after using the body wash, implying that the Black woman was less clean than the White woman. The ad was called inappropriate and racist, and many consumers responded by boycotting Dove products altogether.

Dove quickly removed the post and tweeted an immediate apology, saying it "missed the mark in representing women of color thoughtfully."

And maybe that's the primary lesson we can take away from all this. Recognize that, despite your best efforts, mistakes are going to happen, but how you respond to that mistake is what's going to make *all* the difference.

If you refuse to admit the mistake, try covering it up, or ignore it altogether, the truth will eventually come out—especially given the reach that social media plays in the world today. This will result in even more people being angry at you, and could arguably have a significant negative impact on your bottom line.

However, acknowledging the mistake, apologizing for it, and finding some way to quickly make amends can go a long way to providing damage control and enabling you to move on. Done properly, you might even turn that negative event into a more positive future opportunity.

There are a variety of ways to make amends too. It might be as simple as a mea culpa from the CEO. Or some type of offer to those who were directly impacted by the company's shortfall.

However, if you're looking to *really* turn the situation around, create some kind of cause-related marketing program where every unit sold generates positive financial and PR results for both you and an appropriate nonprofit.

Given that so many major companies have screwed up, why not learn from their lessons so that you can get the benefits without the hit to your own bottom line?

FOOD FOR THOUGHT: If your business makes a mistake, acknowledge it publicly, apologize, and find some way to quickly make amends ...then move on.

55 Years Shot to Hell!

In 2014 the Volkswagen brand stood in the public's opinion for quality, honesty, and customer commitment. They were known for the value of German engineering, instilling feelings of confidence and precision in everything the driver touched. They talked about saying "no" to cars that weren't perfect.

The company's reputation was worth $23 billion in goodwill alone, and VW had become the world's most profitable car manufacturer. Then greed, stupidity, and bad management guaranteed it was all lost . . . *virtually overnight!*

My mother used to tell me, "You spend years building a good reputation and can wipe it out in an instant." I'll confess I didn't always understand what Mom meant . . . until 2015. That was when the Environmental Protection Agency revealed that for six years Volkswagen had been cheating on emissions testing for its diesel cars.

Admittedly, I'm not an automotive engineer, but I *am* a consumer. And when I learned that the cars' computers could detect when they were being tested and temporarily alter how their engines worked, I knew I was being lied to.

Because any simpleton instantly knew that this rigging of the system made VW engines appear to be much more efficient than they actually were. Their supposed good fuel economy entitled them to green car subsidies and tax exemptions in the US . . . but none of that was deserved.

In fact, when they weren't being tested, these same engines belched out 40 times as many pollutants.

Naturally, VW got caught because of "Dieselgate." The CEO resigned, 11 million vehicles were recalled, billions of dollars were levied in fines, and there was a huge loss of a reputation for quality, honesty, and ethical business dealings that the company had been building for 55 years. Customers sued, and VW's reputation took a 20-percent hit in surveys.

VW's little stunt also pulled down the reputation of other automakers they owned (Porsche, Audi) and the diesel market overall (BMW, Mercedes), directly leading to a loss of over 104,000 vehicle sales, representing $5.2 billion in revenue in the US alone.

This was all because the EPA relies on legitimate mileage figures for every car or truck sold in America. Consumers use those figures to decide which vehicle to buy.

By rigging the system, VW inflated their expected mileage. Reports of 45–60 MPG actually turned out to be more like half that. These lower (and more honest) anticipated mileage estimates eliminated the primary reasons to buy a VW, ensuring their sales would plummet.

Going into the 2016 car model year, only one out of four vehicle owners was reported to have a positive opinion of Volkswagen following the scandal—a two-thirds drop from before this little escapade. Their stock also fell by two-thirds, and remained there until a few years later, when supply-chain issues caused by a global pandemic inflated the prices of all car manufacturers.

And did I mention that Volkswagen broke lots of laws, which annoyed some very important people, including employees? And how many dealerships went out of business because of these falsehoods?

True, VW wasn't the first car company to have legal, technical, and safety issues. Toyota had a nasty acceleration issue the previous year. And who could forget GM's ignition problem? People died from both companies' situations . . . only it was accidental for Toyota and GM, while VW did it on purpose.

So Toyota and GM recovered fairly quickly. But years later VW was still trying to escape the shadow of this debacle, and the incident has become a textbook example of what *not* to do in business.

Think of that for a moment: Volkswagen spent 55 years creating amazing advertising demonstrating their value and quality. To their credit were award-winning ads touting their supreme quality control and miserly gas usage.

The company successfully used humor to evolve into one of the most-loved and respected brands of all time.

At this writing they've recovered somewhat. Yet consumer and government watchdogs still keep an extra close eye on Volkswagen, believing the leopard doesn't easily change its spots.

While VW's geniuses debate how to spin this one moving forward to get their business back to its previous heights, I nominate my mother as their new CEO.

She's smart, insightful, honest, talented, and probably would have seen this one coming *long* before those boneheads ever did.

An early VW ad trumpeted, "We pluck the lemons; you get the plums."

Maybe, but it sure sounds to me like they've left a sour taste in the mouths of a lot of people.

FOOD FOR THOUGHT: The company's reputation was worth $23 billion in goodwill alone. Then greed, stupidity, and bad management guaranteed it was all lost . . . virtually overnight!

How Could You Sell That Crap?

Recently, I went white-water rafting on the Kern River in Wofford Heights, California. As I live in San Diego, my friends and I had several hours on the road to reach our destination.

And because I'm the kind of guy who pays attention to signage, I got a huge (and somewhat unsettling) surprise driving through Corona, where I spotted a roadside sign reading *PUS*.

Having a twisted sense of humor, I wondered who would want to buy bodily fluids like pus. And were there enough people buying the stuff to actually turn it into a commercial venture requiring signage?

The sign was owned by a company named Performance Utility Supply. They sell hardware to the power and lighting industries. PUS was obviously an acronym for the full company name, but it struck me that somebody didn't completely think that through.

I guessed most of their customers are "manly" men in the construction trade. The company's website photo of an unshaven guy wearing his PUS gear reinforced my suspicion.

The company also had a sexually suggestive line emblazoned on their trucks ("We have more than just pipe to fill your hole.") And though I find this strategy to be both sexist and personally offensive, I am probably not their target customer. Meaning what I think is realistically of no concern to them.

Because, were I their marketing director, about now I'd probably be saying "If this strategy works for PUS, why should anyone argue?"

Still, one has to wonder about the long-term wisdom of this type of gender-based marketing. While women only make up 11 percent of construction workers today, change is inevitable.

Men continue to hold the upper hand in a majority of traditional industries, including logging, mining, agriculture and, of course, construction. The pandemic didn't help women in their cause for total equality, but with 46.6 percent of the current workforce (and 50.1 percent of the overall population) female, it seems safe to conclude that that 11-percent figure must inevitably grow over time.

All of which suggests the eventuality of more women buyers in construction. And, as buyers, another approach will be needed to catch their attention . . . and their dollars.

Anyone who's paying attention recognizes that women oftentimes view the world differently than men. Historically, professional women are less likely to engage in sophomoric hijinks than their male counterparts.

Which all points to women buyers in construction and related trades who will want to be taken seriously and/or probably be offended by the PUS name and marketing strategy. A rebrand at some point is undoubtedly in this company's future.

Naming a business can be tricky, and it's easy to go down the wrong path. Ego, bad taste, sexism, politics, and plain old stupidity can all come into play. Furthermore, the people naming the business are typically too close to the situation and can't see if a problem exists with a particular name. Or they're emotionally attached to the selected name, and are unable to detach themselves long enough to ask themselves if it's their best option.

Had the management of Performance Utility Supply stepped back for a moment to consider "If Charlie was naming his business this way, how would I react?" they might have seen the situation differently.

Asking others who fit their customer profile but aren't connected to the company in any way (meaning they have nothing to win or lose by the outcome of the conversation) what they thought of the name might have also been useful. However, with so many people lacking humility, insight, or self-awareness, this exercise rarely happens successfully.

Things to consider when you're naming your business include:

- How will your audience receive it?
- How will your acronym read?
- Is the name exciting, or a compromise reached to satisfy a committee?
- Does the name say something, or is it just feeding someone's ego?

- Are you just mashing words together in hopes of being clever?
- Do you stand out from the crowd in a good way?
- Are you merely naming the business after the founder or the town you live in?
- Are you using clichés or obscure words?
- Is your spelling funky?
- Can you get a domain to match your company name?
- Are you budgeting enough to brand your name to customers?
- Can you admit if the company name is just wrong?

Finally, are you prepared to rebrand the company in three years if it turns out you've made a bad selection?

Company names should always bring value to the table. They potentially represent equity for the organization, and are that all-important hook that customers grab onto when they're contemplating making a purchase.

Meaning the last thing you want is for customers to be offended when they see your business's name.

FOOD FOR THOUGHT: Naming a business can be tricky, easily going down the wrong path. Ego, bad taste, politics, and plain old stupidity can all come into play.

Being Proud of Lousy Marketing

Made famous by actor Clint Eastwood, the character Dirty Harry Callahan accurately observed, "A man has to know his limitations."

It's a lesson I learned a long time ago: I just can't do everything.

Sure, I stay in my lane, knowing I'm very strong at writing, strategizing, and networking. But I also know I'm terrible when it comes to graphics. I understand that if you give me a pencil, paper, and a ruler, I'd be hard-pressed to draw a straight line.

Which is why I've become an avowed stick-figure guy, roughing something out before handing it to a designer and asking them to make it look pretty. I know I'm going to bring significantly more value to any conversation by focusing on my areas of expertise, while hiring other professionals to do the things I'm weak on.

Apparently, not everyone has gotten the memo with instructions to do the same thing. Consider some of my friends in real estate.

Like every business owner, each real estate agent wants an edge over the competition. Each focuses on specific niches, and has particular marketing needs to address.

And the marketing plans for most realtors include networking, print advertising, social media, website presence, and collateral for drumming up new business.

So far, so good . . . but here's the wrinkle. An overwhelming percentage of small business owners live with the foolish assumption that because they're good at their core competency, then they can do everything themselves. The logic goes "If I know how to make a hat, then I also know how to sell that hat."

Only it's *very* rare for someone to be able to do everything in their business. As an example, a plumber may be good at plumbing and auto mechanics, but lousy at bookkeeping and contracts.

And, in the case of realtors, marketing is typically outside their core competencies. This causes these folks to sometimes miss the target.

So just as I, as a marketing professional, recognize I'm not a plumber, nor should I sell real estate, most real estate professionals should understand that they'll benefit by having a marketing professional help them bridge the gaps in their communications strategies.

Consider, for a moment, Jones Realty. Yes, their name is changed for this story, but their situation is quite real. This firm is currently running an attractive ad in an expensive print publication. To maximize exposure, there's a lightbox in their storefront window in North County San Diego. On the lightbox is this page, torn from the magazine.

Only there's a technical problem they've obviously never considered. The bright background light reveals the ad on the reverse side of the page. Backward. This, in turn, makes the Jones Realty ad in the window unreadable.

The problem is immediately noticeable to anyone walking by the office after dark.

Presenting the ad this way is amateurish, though the problem could have been solved by reprinting the ad on plain magazine stock without anything on the reverse side . . . *then* posting it on the light box.

Too bad nobody at Jones Realty checked the ad or asked for a second opinion.

You might think I'm being persnickety, which is just a fancy way of saying I'm being a pain in the rump. And I'd have probably agreed with that assessment if I hadn't also seen the company's sales brochure, containing these mistakes:

- The personalized cover had a misspelled name on it.
- The market activity map incorrectly identified several street names.
- Property listings referred to streets not identified on the map.
- The preprinted brochure shell was very pretty, but the personalized section (with the actual local listings) looked *terrible*!

Acting as both a marketing professional and columnist, I called the owner of Jones Realty and asked about these issues. Her response: "Okay," without any whiff of concern or contrition.

I thought this odd in such a competitive industry, where agents rely on referrals and long-term relationships. As I'd mentioned my plans to write this column, I figured she had an opportunity to create some positive publicity. Instead, her standoffishness persuaded me that this is someone I'll never want to do business with. You can also be assured I'll persuade my friends not to bother with her either.

If you're a realtor, your success will probably also depend upon extensive networking, pounding the pavement, signage, and generating actual results which, in turn, will lead to more referrals. The collateral, advertising, social media posts, drip campaigns, and websites you'll use to spread the message will help complement your primary efforts.

All of which sounds great on paper. However, if your secondary efforts degrade your primary ones, you've hurt yourself more than helped.

Regular readers know I'm a great believer in business planning, comprehensive follow-through, and sticking to deadlines.

Seeing these kinds of issues in such a hyper-competitive environment reinforces the importance of mapping out strategy, solid implementation, and as my first-grade teacher regularly reminded me, checking your work.

After all, you only get one chance to make that first impression, right?

And, if someone contacts you and says, "Hey, you made a mistake on your website, LinkedIn post, etc.," be gracious, say thank you, and look carefully at what's being pointed out. Then fix it!

Because you never know what your marketing looks like to members of the public. And, if someone is kind enough to volunteer to help you clean up your messaging, they're signaling a willingness to help you open doors with potentially big long-term impacts on your business.

FOOD FOR THOUGHT: You're usually better off hiring specialists for particular services, enabling you to focus on what you do best.

Tattoo That Tagline onto Your Head!

The tagline—10 words or less telling customers what your company stands for—may make the difference between success and failure for a business.

A properly developed and supported slogan or tagline will be memorable. And because of its ability to jump into the buyer's mind when they are ready to make a purchase, a good tagline can easily change a consumer's buying habits.

Those habits, in turn, can help influence the buying decisions of others.

The tagline should be a key part of your company's brand—something you imprint on every brochure, coffee mug, or website. It tells how you're different, and it needs a great deal of thought to get it right. Furthermore, once it's settled upon, it should not be changed unless you're doing an overall rebranding effort. And it should be shouted from the rooftops regularly and often.

A startling number of business owners don't understand why they'll benefit from having a tagline as part of their branding effort. To address this question, we should turn to the world of politics to learn a lesson.

Since 1840, every presidential candidate with the best slogan has won the race. When neither had a good slogan, it was a close election. Slogans have been used to motivate people to go to war. And they've persuaded folks to move into new neighborhoods and across countries.

So you tell me . . . is a good tagline important to your success?

As you may already know, the average American adult is bombarded by close to 10,000 marketing messages every 24 hours. But our brains are wired to remember the unusual. "Got Milk?" sunk in because it was short, pithy, had personality, and was easily memorable. Repetition and clever imagery helped as well.

Which suggests a short phrase with personality stays in the brain long after the logo or company name is forgotten.

Of course, it's not easy to explain your message in most short phrases. Probably 98 percent of the taglines in the marketplace fall flat because they lack personality, attitude, or unique promise. They're not well thought out and don't tell a story.

When you consider how important a story is to make yourself memorable to a customer, that tagline becomes the linchpin to your communications efforts.

My guess is you'll find most of these lackadaisical phrases have been created by oversized committees with artificial deadlines, almost guaranteeing failure before you've started. Memorable expressions like Coke's "It's the Real Thing" or FedEx's "Absolutely, Positively Overnight!" didn't come about by turning a faucet. They most certainly didn't come about because a committee decided to be brilliant or pithy.

And, at the risk of putting *too* fine a point on it, taglines usually aren't easy to get right. I learned this when it took my team four years to get our agency's tagline right.

It's the same way you need to be looking at your own branding. You need the right players in the room, willing to stay on task until you have success . . . and without some artificial deadline. You need to be willing to set your ego aside, yell at each other a bit, and recognize that you all share the same objective.

Then, once you've found success, your tagline should be used with every promotion, every radio or TV ad, every direct mail campaign. Even as your promotions change, the same tagline should be used—especially if it announces something about your company that competitors can't easily duplicate.

Yes, you knew I was going to say it: Your slogan should demonstrate your unique selling proposition.

Finally, as you develop your tagline, remember to use bold words to help you stand out from the crowd a bit more. Because it's okay to have an attitude in your tagline. In truth, tagline success almost *demands* an attitude.

So go buy that bottle of Three-Buck Chuck to get that flash of inspiration. Bandy about a lot of ideas to find a few choice words that sum up who and what your business is about. Let it reflect your personality, your business philosophy, and your aspirations.

Because if you can create a phrase that entertains, inspires, or enlightens, your business is almost certain to benefit over time.

———————————————

FOOD FOR THOUGHT: Know your audience, your message, and your unique features. Together, they should lead you toward a brilliant tagline.

Value from a Soft Launch

It's scary to speak with a long-term client and realize they don't know the services you provide.

It was a startling discovery that I made when Craig, a client of several years, announced he was having a new website built. As my agency had been handling his advertising, collateral, publicity, and newsletters for quite a long time, I was understandably dismayed to learn we hadn't even been invited to the discussion.

Yet when I confronted him about the matter, Craig's response was to laugh and say, "I didn't even know you did that!"

What part of "Full-service marketing communications agency" didn't he understand?

Regardless of what you sell, an impactful brand must speak to your customers, staff, media, and other audiences.

Without successfully communicating who and what your business is, the company (and brand) loses impact and risks becoming irrelevant. Even growing businesses will eventually stagnate.

Sometimes it's hard to recognize the necessity for a brand refresh. We get into our daily rhythm, hustling for sales and servicing clientele, and kind of put our branding efforts on autopilot.

However, every business needs to periodically revisit their public image, and my marketing agency was no different.

The truth is that for 20 years we'd argued internally over the logo. It was a set of stairs suggesting building markets, and we'd developed it at the agency's inception.

Over time we'd had countless debates about whether my hat represented the agency or my personal branding. Invariably, the conversation concluded with my partner insisting the hat was *my* brand and the stairs were the agency's. Yet, given my prominence in the business, I argued the hat represented both me *and* the agency.

Then I had that root-shaking conversation with Craig, and came away convinced our clients didn't understand who we were, what we did, or why we mattered.

Something obviously needed to change!

My team and I spent the next several weeks strategizing extensively to revitalize our professional persona. We recognized that we were a marketing consultancy with *lots* of connections, rather than being just another advertising agency.

It was a subtle, but important, difference.

A new website was designed and written to accurately reflect this revised image. Our revitalized message revealed previously hidden strengths.

Then a new logo was designed. And, in case you were wondering, it *did* incorporate the hat (we got rid of the stairs). Then we quickly freshened up our letterhead, invoices, and newsletter templates to reveal our new image and message to the world.

Today I'll confess we quietly launched the new website (marketbuilding.com) six weeks ago so we had time to work out any kinks. Language was tweaked and images replaced until everything was perfect.

Perfect—yeah, *that's* a laugh! Frustratingly, this six-month project took well over a year. Serves me right for being such a stickler.

And it's not really finished, either. After all, websites take on a life of their own, and need to be constantly fed new material . . . lest they get lonely when nobody visits them.

But with today's arrival of our second round of snappy new business cards we're ready for prime time. Sadly, the first round had to be replaced when we discovered the new tagline line was wrong, and the mistake hadn't been caught during the proofreading stage.

Color me exasperated!

If it's been years that you've been using your current business image, a new look may also benefit you. It'll allow you to clarify your message while reintroducing yourself to people so used to having you there that they don't even see you anymore.

They are, in fact, taking you for granted.

Because here's what it all boils down to: If you're not telling your story properly, you can't expect customers to do it for you. You need to spell out for them who you are and why you're important to them, their business, and their associates.

Regularly investing in your brand will bring tangible positive results to your bottom line. And a fresh look will demonstrate your value, differentiate you once again from the competition, and encourage customers to champion you.

Things are slow right now, right? Put the time to good use by giving your organization a brand-new look . . . and a brighter future.

And even if things aren't slow for you, do yourself a favor and periodically ask a few trusted clients, friends, and associates to describe what you do . . . without them first looking at your website or social media.

You might find the results of the conversation to be both enlightening . . . *and* disturbing.

FOOD FOR THOUGHT: A new image for your organization may allow you to clarify your message and reintroduce yourself to people so used to you that they don't even see you anymore.

Presenting Your Business Pleasantly

Years ago I learned that breaking bread with clients engenders better relations and smooths over potential conflicts. With that in mind, more days than not I find myself doing business over coffee or a sandwich.

Of course it's not the coffee or meal, per se, but rather the opportunity it provides to relax and speak more candidly. Arguably, coffee meetings are more effective than meetings that involve alcohol. After all, I can only do one or two meetings per day involving alcohol, while I can do six at coffee shops.

Which is probably why my attorney suggested last week that a contract negotiation we were engaged in should take place over coffee.

There's an old joke that goes like this:

Patron: Waiter, what is this cockroach doing in my coffee?

Waiter: The backstroke, sir.

Of course, that's ridiculous, since everyone knows cockroaches are famous for doing the butterfly stroke.

Nevertheless, here I was at the local coffee shop meeting with my attorney. Imagine our surprise when the Orkin man (in full bug-killing regalia) strolled through the store full of customers.

And he was there to work, not socialize.

As a recovering New Yorker, I wasn't particularly surprised. I understand food establishments and insects naturally go together. Show me a restaurant and I'll show you a bug infestation . . . just by turning on the kitchen lights.

However, not everyone recognizes this relationship. Lots of folks assume the A rating in the window certifies there are no pests . . . which is nearly impossible.

Still, having an exterminator in full view of customers called to attention the presence of vermin around the scene I was previously enjoying.

EW!

Why not just stand on the counter with a megaphone and scream, "The cockroaches are taking over the world. RUN FOR YOUR LIVES!!!!!"?

Had the manager thought more strategically, he would have considered this scenario through customers' eyes. The exterminator could have visited the night before. Or come in through a back door. Or shown up with his uniform in a bag and changed in the back.

In short, anything that would not have emphasized the presence of horrific bugs to a roomful of paying clientele.

Then, whatever the problem, it would have been resolved with customers none the wiser.

True, the Orkin visit was potentially preemptive. However, the high visibility of this messenger of insect death sent an extremely negative message. I, for one, haven't returned to that particular coffee shop since.

And yes, this is even as I recognize that every other coffee shop I patronize is guaranteed to have the exact same problem.

Regardless of what you sell, your business may also have unpleasant issues that must be dealt with. Exterminators, trash removal, dirty laundry . . . these are all facts of life.

Yet it makes no sense to build and advertise a sparkling shop with quality products, get your location and pricing *just* right, and train your employees to properly greet customers . . . only to ruin it by broadcasting something that's ugly or distasteful. In a case like this, a little discretion can go a *long* way!

Which is why, even if it means spending a few extra dollars to have the service provided after hours, I'd call it a justified cost of doing business.

If it means the boss has to come in on a day off to quietly tend to undesirable details . . . such is the joy of being the boss.

Look, I'm a big boy. I know there are bugs, mice, or whatever in the kitchen. They're there regardless of the traps, the cats, or the poison.

But when I'm out for either a social or business event, I don't need to be reminded about it.

Because like many business owners, I sometimes get stuck behind my desk and yearn for a change of scenery. And if I'm coming to your shop to break bread with someone, I need you to send me a message that your shop is clean.

Bottom line: If that coffee shop with the Orkin man had done that— even though deep down I'd have known they were putting a spin on the story—I'd still be going there.

Instead, my attorney and I will never see that shop the same way again.

Which means though we've talked about revisiting that establishment due to its great location, maybe a donut and coffee at his office will work better for us from now on.

Even if we can't solve all the world's problems, at least we won't have to observe them while we're enjoying our conversation.

FOOD FOR THOUGHT: I know there are bugs, mice, or whatever in every commercial kitchen. But when I'm out for either a social or business event, I don't need to be reminded about it.

Who's Really the Best?

===========================

When starting to work with any new client, I'll typically ask one simple question: "Why should I buy from *you*?"

If their answer is "Great quality," "Wonderful service," "Good prices," or something similar, I'll usually give them a raspberry and point out that the competitor down the street is probably saying the *exact* same words.

Which means the question "Why should I buy from *you*?" remains unanswered.

Over the past few years, between supply-chain issues, COVID lockdowns, and sky-high interest rates, the economy has been going through some very interesting gyrations.

Which forces us to address the $64 question: Why are so many companies continuing to take the lazy way out and either are not marketing themselves, or are following a cookie-cutter strategy?

I'll go a step further and ask why so many of them just do whatever the competition's doing, making little effort to grab attention or demonstrate what makes them superior to the guy down the street.

For obvious reasons, none of these "solutions" adequately motivates sales prospects to buy. After all, if I can't tell the difference between you and the guy down the street, why should I buy from either of you?

There's a wonderful scene in the movie *Elf* where Will Ferrell's character sees a neon sign in a New York City coffee shop's window that proclaims they serve "The World's Best Cup of Coffee." Ferrell's character takes this sign at its word, though the coffee is, from all appearances, terrible.

Most customers aren't as naïve as Buddy the Elf, and you can't count on them to take your word for it merely because you say you're good at what you do.

Consider the plumbing truck that drove by my house today. On its side was the phrase "You've tried all the rest: now use the best." I've also seen pizza parlors and coffee shops that use the exact same phrase to "distinguish" themselves.

Yet this appalling lack of marketing creativity provides zero reasons for me to believe them. Furthermore, what claim do any of these businesses have to being called "the best"? I've never seen my friends enamored enough of them to post about them on Facebook or Yelp.

In fact, these businesses—plumber, coffee shop, pizza parlor, etc.—offer absolutely no proof that they're even qualified to be in business, let alone to assert they're superior to their industry counterparts.

Rather than using the same words everyone else seems to use to stand out from the crowd, these businesses might have done better had they invested some time and effort to develop an original tagline reinforcing their sales message and moving the customer closer to actually buying from them. Actually acquiring testimonials and promoting them would help too.

But it's the tagline—a phrase of under 10 words providing specific reasons for the customer to hand over their hard-earned cash—that supports complementary messaging in social media, websites, collateral, and all other media and tends to stick in the customer's mind longer.

That's why I see KFC and think "It's Finger Lickin' Good." And I think of Coke when I see the phrase "It's the Real Thing."

So what kind of subconscious thinking does "tagline laziness" inspire in a consumer? "Bare-bones tagline? Bare-bones service? Not with *my* money! I'll shop elsewhere."

Now I'm the last one to suggest that putting your company's personality and style into a brief statement is an easy task. For proof, I need look no further than my own ad agency's tagline: "Unique marketing solutions. Profitable results."

It took us four years to develop that simple five-word phrase. However, once we put it together, that phrase went *everyplace*: onto business cards, CD labels, PowerPoint presentations, newsletters, our website, and every other marketing tool we've used since.

Because with that phrase people immediately began to know what they'd get for their money when they're working with us. And there's no chance we'll ever be mistaken for a plumber.

Regardless of what you sell, you too will undoubtedly benefit from having a snappy phrase that instantly identifies what you do and sell.

But do yourself a favor and don't try to create one in a vacuum, as doing so virtually guarantees mediocrity. Rather, gather a team of trusted staff and friends to spitball ideas, and don't stop until you come to a consensus.

Then, when you think your selling phrase is ready for prime time, ask current customers for their opinions. Take their advice, even if it means starting again from scratch.

Because these friends of your company are telling you what strangers—the people not buying from you—are also thinking.

FOOD FOR THOUGHT: Don't try to create a quality tagline in a vacuum, as doing so virtually guarantees mediocrity.

Marketing with a Hidden Message

A few years back I had a client who needed a new logo. "Make it like the one they use at FedEx," he said.

Copyright issues and the client being in a completely different industry aside, his meaning was clear: He liked the idea of a hidden message.

In 1957, Vance Packard published *The Hidden Persuaders*, exploring consumer motivation and subliminal advertising used to manipulate expectations and induce desire for products.

This classic, pioneering, and prescient work revealed how advertisers use psychological methods to tap into our unconscious desires in order to "persuade" us to buy the products they are selling.

And for those not familiar with the FedEx logo, it has a hidden message (a white arrow) between the last two letters. This tricky optical illusion stands for speed, accuracy, striving for perfection, and perseverance in achieving goals.

There are dozens of logos with similarly hidden messages, including Amazon (making customers smile with everything from *A* to *Z*), Baskin Robbins (31 Flavors), and Wendy's (notice "MOM" in the ruff at her neck).

These subliminal messages reinforce the overall ideas each of these companies are trying to impart.

Perhaps this explains why, as a youth, I heard rumors that the dots in Ritz crackers spelled out "SEX." While I never bought into the idea, it's obvious that an active imagination could make it appear legitimate.

This is also probably why the TV commercial for the LA injury law firm, whose last seven digits are 8-0-0-0-0-0-0, caught my attention. Every time they say the number (including in their musical tagline) they say, "eight million."

This is a marketing column, so I won't debate the value of any law firm's services. However, from a marketing perspective it's nothing less than brilliant to subtly impart the message: "Hire us, and you'll get millions of dollars."

Regardless of what you sell, you may also be able to use subliminal messaging in your own marketing materials. The Pittsburgh Zoo does it with animals tucked into their logo graphics. Magnum ice cream bars use packaging with an image that (at first glance) looks like a naked torso. The list is endless.

Furthermore, it's hard to ignore a hidden message once you're aware of it. If you've seen the Tostitos logo, with its two people dipping a chip into salsa, you understand my meaning.

Taking this step can be worth considering as you examine your own business's messaging. Whether in your advertising, tagline, logo, or phone number, ask what you are saying to potential customers.

Plus it's important to remember that *you* aren't the customer. You may be too close to the issue to see if there are any problems presented by your communications tools.

Which is why, prior to any launch, you need to examine the hidden message you're trying to impart. Is it clear, clever, and subtle . . . or is it *so* clever that it's completely hidden unless someone points it out to a customer? And does it speak to your audience, your product (or service), and your organization's personality?

As with so many of your marketing materials, and to be sure you're achieving your objective, have someone unrelated to the business review your message to ensure it's accomplishing its objectives. Better yet, bring a few trusted customers into the process to help guide your thinking and the final result.

Having good communications is critical to any business's success, and imparting an idea that constantly reinforces itself—logo, jingle, tagline—can have a huge impact on your bottom line.

And while my erstwhile client knew he wanted something clever, he had no idea *what* he wanted or needed. It was only by my speaking with some of his clientele that we were able to determine what imagery made the most sense.

Meaning we can learn from his initial idea of looking both inside and outside his industry for ideas. See what appeals to you, and note *why* it's so appealing.

Then take a lesson from our legal friends in Los Angeles . . . because the right image can really get your phones ringing.

———————————————

FOOD FOR THOUGHT: The right image can really get your phones ringing.

Should You Be a Sexy Blonde?

Does your business have a personality?

If so, what is it? Are you playful like Ben & Jerry's? Or buttoned up like Brooks Brothers?

This is an important question, because the personality your business adopts will be reflected in your website, collateral, social media, blogs, and . . . well, you get the idea.

So take a minute, gather up all your messaging materials, and consider the overall image you want to present to the world. Are you trying to be young and hip, like Apple? Generous like the YMCA? Somber and/ or boring like . . . just about everyone else?

The problem is most organizations never even consider this question. Hence, they lack an image that runs consistently through their messaging. One firm I know uses great graphics for their business card and letterhead, then goes off in two totally different directions for their website and their public presentations.

Their messaging on the website is fun and (arguably) frivolous. Their social media is statistics one day, cartoony the next. Their newsletter tone is fairly serious.

They are, in fact, all over the place!

This lack of consistency subconsciously suggests that the business owners don't know who they really are. Which means that even though this firm provides great service, has a targeted (and unique) selling proposition, and is very competitively priced, there's no one handle for folks to grab onto.

They can fix the problem, but they obviously need to spend some time focusing on the issue. For example, management at this company might decide to continue the silly messaging and graphics into their social media, PowerPoint, blog, and newsletter. In short, the business's communications needs to echo a particular tone at every turn.

With that consistency in place, over time they'll become known for their graphic imagery and as silly guys who take their business seriously.

There are lots of ways for you to express your company's personality, including:

- **Sound.** Let's say you like Chinese stuff, and build your branding around a Chinese style, fonts and all. The website, social media, collateral, etc. all incorporate lots of red and gold, dragons, and similar imagery, and every time the company's name comes up, people hear a Chinese gong. Even if you're a White guy with absolutely no background in the Chinese culture, customers will eventually envision the company every time they hear a gong. Call it Pavlovian marketing, if you will.

  One could even argue that the potential visibility brought on by bad publicity over charges of cultural appropriation may only help expand your visibility.

- **Personal branding.** As you know, my firm is small, so I've built my brand around wearing a Panama hat. It helps folks pick me out of the crowd, and people seeing anyone wearing my kind of hat immediately think of me and my marketing agency.

- **Create a character.** The Geico Gecko's a prime example. This computer-animated creature sells Geico's insurance services while saying some pretty outrageous things. Because the audience is amused, they listen to the sales message . . . which was the objective all along.

- **License a character.** For over 30 years, MetLife Insurance was associated with Snoopy. This helped the company target the nostalgia many of its customers felt for the *Peanuts* gang. It was only after much of that generation had transitioned from being the primary buyers of insurance that Snoopy was retired.

- **Celebrity endorsements.** Having a sports or entertainment figure as your public face lets you ride their coattails and reach their fan base with your message. However, using a real person runs the risk of them having an accident, committing a crime, abusing drugs or alcohol, or otherwise potentially sullying your image . . . and your investment.

All of which means you have options, though they all seem to come down to the initial question: What's the personality of your business? Once you know who you are, you'd be wise to invest some time to determine how best to demonstrate your unique personality through your marketing materials.

And at every stage of the process, of course, your objective should always be to show customers how enjoyable, serious, or profitable it is to do business with you.

You might be surprised at how successful you can be by using that personality to be recognized, and how seeing that imagery automatically reminds people about who you are and what you sell.

FOOD FOR THOUGHT: Creating a personality for your business, and systematically inserting it into all your communications materials, is virtually a guarantee of a fatter bottom line.

Say the Secret Word

On his 1950s game show *You Bet Your Life*, Groucho Marx used to reward contestants who guessed the secret word of the day.

Guests would come out to banter with Mr. Marx, usually ending up on the wrong end of his never-ending string of one-liners. If anyone said that particular show's special word, a stuffed duck bearing a striking resemblance to Mr. Marx (cigar and all) would drop down on a string and give them a hundred dollars.

The show was a huge success.

Yet, even though prizes have increased in value and the times overall have changed somewhat, contestants in today's business world are also rewarded when they determine the secret word of the day.

Consider the Magic Castle in Los Angeles, where the secret word is *exclusivity*. Established in 1963 in a Victorian era mansion, this home of the Academy of Magical Arts sits in the Hollywood Hills as the equivalent of Broadway for the Merlin set.

Behind these walls, patrons are entertained by the finest magicians in the world. Virtuosos perfect their craft and their patter before live audiences, and experience prestidigitation sure to confound even the most careful observer.

We're talking serious magic here … not Harry Potter.

Visiting the Castle, in fact, is an experience unlike any other. It's got an upscale atmosphere, a professional dress code, and despite (or perhaps because of) periodic scandals, is largely considered to be one of the entertainment industry's hottest tickets.

Furthermore, you can't just walk in off the street to attend an event at this private club; entry is by invitation only. You must be a member (there's a waiting list with hundreds of names on it) or a guest of a member to access the secret panel in the lobby and find yourself within the massive—and impressive—club beyond.

Jacket and tie are required, and the atmosphere is what my mother would have called chic.

Now, anyone who has entered through this secret panel knows the password ("Open Sesame") is supposed to make you smile—as it did for us when we visited the club one Friday night and left there sated by fine food and intelligent conversation.

The menu was *not* cheap! And, for the record, we still remain totally confounded about how that lemon got into that empty cup not 12 inches from my nose.

Stay with me for a minute and allow me to elaborate the term *exclusive*. Joining the club costs $5,000 and involves jumping through numerous hoops. Despite that, there's that mile-long waiting list.

Do you get where I'm going here? The Magic Castle has a reputation for rarified air combined with high prices . . . and there's an endless line of people wanting to buy their offerings.

Following a similar strategy, my friend Dave tells people he only takes on three clients at a time. Period. If you want to hire him, you may have to wait in line.

Now think about Rolls-Royce: handmade, limited quantities, negligible recalls . . . and *very* desirable.

Anyone paying attention has noticed the patterns: that a reputation for quality and limited availability drives up desirability. It's also playing on FOMO—the Fear of Missing Out.

Meaning it may be time to examine your own business. Regardless of what you sell, you, too, can benefit from an image of exclusivity.

After all, if customers see your offerings as a commodity, you'll quickly find yourself in a race to the bottom. Price alone will determine whether you make the sale, since people can probably go down the street and buy what you sell for less.

And don't kid yourself: Many customers *will* go down the street to save that $2.

Or they'll come to you with questions before making their purchases online. Sometimes they'll shop online while they browse through your store.

It's rude, I know. It's also true.

However, if the buying public recognizes they can't get your offerings anyplace else, several things happen:

- You eliminate competition.
- You become more desirable.
- You can raise prices.

Face it: If you've got the only lemonade stand in town on a hot day, you're going to get lots of business, even if you charge above market rates.

And, taken a step further, even if you're not the only one who provides what you do, exuding the perception of exclusivity increases your desirability.

Making your business's secret word *Lucrative*.

═══════════════════

FOOD FOR THOUGHT: A reputation for limited availability drives up desirability.

How'm I Supposed to Find You?

T here's a company in Little Rock, Arkansas, called Good Old Days Foods.

"As homemade as you can buy!" their website proclaims, adding "Maintaining the flavor of the past with a unique homemade appearance."

Sounds wonderful, doesn't it? I discovered their products when visiting Baron's grocery store in Rancho Bernardo, California. And inside the package I found a pie that was tasty and priced fairly.

But being inquisitive and tending to view everything in the world through a marketing filter, I also examined the packaging quite closely. *That* is when I got confused.

I was amazed to find no address, phone number, or website information anywhere on the container or wrapper. The only reason I located their website was because I did an extensive search for it.

These folks obviously don't want anyone finding them, but for the life of me I couldn't understand why.

I know . . . I know . . . if I want to buy more, I can just go back to Baron's, right? But what if Baron's stops carrying their line of products?

Besides, as the owner of a small ad agency, I'm always on the lookout for potential clients. And from what I saw on the package, it looked to me like these guys might benefit from my firm's services.

Yet, setting my own mercenary instincts aside, I found myself wondering how the typical consumer learns more about this obscure food producer.

Anyone truly interested in learning the 10 reasons to buy GODF's frozen fruit cobbler would need to Google this Arkansas firm's website, then search the site hoping to find additional information. There they'd discover a small handful of desserts and side dishes available for purchase . . . assuming your local grocer carries them, of course.

But the physical product itself had no recipes or serving suggestions. No promotions or collateral were attached, either. Nor was there a display of any kind, but hey ... you can't have everything, right?

Still, the question remains—why is the company making it difficult for me to contact them? I mean, these are apple dumplings we're talking about—not state secrets.

It's true some companies don't want you calling them, forcing customers to use email and allowing them to control the conversation. Names like eBay and Amazon jump to mind.

And their need for that control makes perfect sense when you consider the sheer volume of customers (and the avalanche of anticipated callers) for an operation like Amazon.

But Good Old Days Foods is no Amazon, and they should (arguably) want customer dialogue. True, they only seem to want brokers, but they're not making it easy for *anyone* to find them just by looking at the package.

Admittedly, their seven-page website provides six ways to contact them, including the plant's street address. But they're making me (or food brokers who discover them by accident) work awfully hard to find that information.

Sounds to me less like a control issue and more like poor design and planning for their packaging.

It's a funny thing about our economy. Regardless of inflation, interest rates, politics, and all the rest, businesses continue to open, close, and jostle for ways to build their bottom line.

Which is why, as you read these words, businesses left and right are churning in an effort to gain customers. They improve their chances by making it easy for prospective customers to reach out and hand over their money.

After all, regardless of your industry, you've got competition. And the winner, in the long run, is going to be whoever makes it as easy and pleasant as possible to do business with them.

These guys in Arkansas apparently didn't get that memo.

When I first entered the business world, my dad told me you never know when someone will want to work with you. And Mom's words about making a good first impression are always swirling around in my brain.

Meaning if you're making it difficult for someone to find you or work with you, there's a subtle message that you'll also be difficult to work with later. And because of the preponderance of competitors available in every category, and the simplicity of communications available these days, just a whiff of trouble is going to send hordes of potential business scurrying for the hills.

Translation: They'll never know about your great customer service. Or those terrific promotions you're planning to run next year.

In these days of hustling for more, more, more, being difficult is the *last* message you want possible customers to come away with before they've even gotten in your front door. Or, for that matter, after they're working with you.

The good news: There's still time to review and adjust your next marketing campaign. Remember to make it easy for customers to find you, work with you, and want to refer you to their friends.

Which brings us full circle to this: As you're reviewing your own marketing materials—product packaging, collateral, website, print ads, social media, etc.—be sure you have easily accessible contact information everywhere.

After all, you never know where someone's going to be looking with an eye toward doing business with you.

FOOD FOR THOUGHT: Being difficult is the *last* message you want possible customers to come away with before they've even gotten in your front door.

What the Hell Are We Talking About?

Many marketing professionals mistakenly assume that, because they understand something, everyone else understands it as well. This misconception frequently leads to confused customers and lost sales.

Take as an example an advertisement I heard on a San Diego radio station a while back for a local firm named Battiata Real Estate. The ad referred listeners to the company's website for more information about the firm and their services and property listings.

The only problem was they never spelled out the address. Was it *badeeatta*? Maybe it was *bad-d-adda*.

Now I don't know about you, but my days are usually *way* too busy to spend chunks of time trying to track down an advertiser's website. Especially in an industry like real estate, where it seems you can't swing a dead cat without hitting 10 agents on any given day.

Furthermore, most home buyers or sellers prefer to work with someone with whom they already have an existing relationship. Which brings it all down to this: With so much competition for my attention, you'd better make it as easy as possible for me to find you, or I'm moving on to the next guy ... and quickly.

Battiata (I looked it up) could have resolved this matter quickly and painlessly by spelling out their name (twice) in this same radio spot. This tweak would have instantly made them more accessible and user-friendly, while eating up a mere 5 seconds from their 30-second ad.

Furthermore, I'm pretty sure I wasn't the only person to gripe about this issue, yet the ad would still pop up periodically. This suggests Battiata either had an ad that worked ... or they just didn't care.

Of course, if the ad worked well as a selling tool, more power to them. I recognize that I don't know everything, and we can chalk this entire discussion up to my being a puffed-up bag of wind.

But the ad never appeared to run frequently enough to generate a steady flow of business. This, then, suggests to me that someone in a position to change things didn't know better . . . or didn't give a hoot.

Which forces the question: Would listeners take time to seek them out in such a scenario?

I think not. After all, if a company makes me work this hard just to find them, what kind of a nightmare might they be like if we actually signed a contract?

True, anyone willing to track down the website must be serious about doing business with them, right? And since I'm basically a lazy guy, I've self-selected myself out as a bad prospect. It's an interesting sales strategy, though I'm not sure that's what they had in mind.

Yet if they wanted to increase response from their ads, they might have also considered:

- Buying longer ads to enable the simplicity I crave in my messaging. Naturally, this would translate to spending more money or buying fewer spots within the same budget.
- Producing shorter ads. A shorter message would have allowed time to spell out the company name. This assumes, though, that it wasn't the boss or someone else high on the totem pole who wrote the original ad copy. In my experience, many of these types of folks have egos that don't allow for anyone editing or otherwise meddling with their "creative product."
- Buying an easily understood domain (like BRE.com) to improve listener comprehension.

Assuming others know what you know (industry terminology, a name, street, or website domain) can be as bad for business as making it difficult for customers to give you their money.

Because regardless of what you're selling, there's lots of competition for every dollar. Make it hard for most customers to do business with you and they're *gone*! Getting them back will typically be challenging at best, impossible at worst.

So let me offer a friendly suggestion: As you plan your next year's marketing efforts, see if you've made it easy for prospective customers to find you and do business with you. Check with a few trusted customers to see if your message resonates with them. And make sure your website is easy to negotiate while providing a positive customer experience.

To ensure your messaging really works, also ask a disinterested friend or two to review your materials. After all, the message you intend to send may be *very* different from the message your audience receives.

Then, once everyone is convinced your communications are clear, get the word out loudly and often. Invest an adequate budget and work your plan to the maximum.

The next 12 months promise to be good for a great many people, and you need to get ready for it now. Start by making it easy for folks to want to work with you.

It's certain to make a big difference in your bottom line.

FOOD FOR THOUGHT: Make it as easy as possible for customers to give you their money.

Standing Out among Realtors

Confucius said, "May you always live in interesting times." And *these* are some *very* interesting times in the real estate market.

As I write this, interest rates are on the rise again, scaring countless would-be homebuyers out of the marketplace. Lots of realtors are also dropping out of the business, as the effort and required investment to get clientele and close deals is getting more intense.

The problem, of course, is that realtors, mortgage brokers, and a host of other service providers along the chain between home buyer and seller don't get paid until a deal is done. This means they're obliged to work on speculation, and if a deal falls through ... well, they're stuck for the investment they've made.

Naturally, when interest rates drop again, the sheer volume of realtors will increase exponentially. The increased competition and noise will make it more challenging to acquire the returning clientele.

Such is the nature of this particular beast.

If you're a realtor, you should be asking why any homeowner should want to work with you under any circumstances. Sure, you'll say you provide great service, get higher selling prices, and sell faster than other realtors.

Only every realtor I've ever met basically says the same things. So again I ask why anyone should deal with *you*?

Now consider this: I know several dozen real estate agents. Some I know professionally, and others socially. Yet I don't work with any of them.

Because on the first day of every new season, my bride and I get a personal note from the woman through whom we bought our house several years ago. Though we have no plans to buy or sell again anytime soon, she stays in touch.

Unsurprisingly, she remains top of our minds. She invests a few dollars and a few minutes every few months, and thus ensures our loyalty.

Buyers and sellers typically contact whomever they worked with previously when it comes to their next real estate transaction. This makes sense, as there's already an existing relationship there, and trust has been established through a major transaction.

So unless that realtor totally messes up, or leaves the business, they've usually already got the inside track before the conversation starts.

And even if it's been years since the last transaction, that realtor stands to potentially make tens of thousands of dollars merely by providing a gentle nudge and staying in touch.

Of course, you may want more business than referrals provide. Or you haven't yet developed a pipeline of relationships, because your status as an outsider puts you at a disadvantage.

Catching a homeowner's attention may be as easy as knocking on the door, explaining that you specialize in one particular neighborhood's real estate issues, and offering yourself as a free information resource. Not pressuring an owner may help them think positively of you when your postcard or newsletter arrives.

Or sponsor a neighborhood garage sale with no strings attached. Pick a spring Saturday morning and you may easily see 100 homeowners participating in the event. They'll all sport your sign in their yards, and your job will be to advertise the event and bring donuts and coffee to the sales sites. Prospective clients probably won't automatically toss your postcards and other promotional materials in the future.

Want more? Break down walls of mistrust by focusing on any group's special needs. For example, I've seen realtors who declare themselves specialists in particular age groups or ethnic markets. They provide seminars with information about the financing markets, job or educational opportunities, reverse mortgages, or relocation.

Or offer ideas on your website regarding healthy lifestyles, exercise, or travel. Just don't use the generic event schedules or same newsletter services every other realtor seems to use.

Finding success may even be as simple as developing a solid tagline and call to action in your existing communications materials.

Whether there's a sour economy or an overload of competitors, you must find some way to call attention to yourself. Just doing things the same old way will only generate the same old results . . . if you're lucky.

So determine what's unique about you and your business, and find a way to effectively communicate that difference. Take your dog with you on sales calls, always wear red, or sport an easily identifiable hat. If you have an intense interest in trivia, position yourself as the person with all the answers. You get the idea.

Next, take a hard look at other realtors in your area and see what they're doing. If everyone says they're good and friendly, think about ads announcing you're grumpy and cranky. Again, be different to ensure you stand out from the crowd.

Simultaneously market yourself and press current customers for testimonials and referrals. A client is happiest within 30 days of the sale, so always get a letter or email (*fast!*) touting how wonderful you are. Or ask them to post kind words about you on Google, Yelp, NextDoor, or Facebook.

And if someone *really* likes you, offer to sponsor a housewarming party in their new home. A lawn sign with your logo should congratulate the new owners.

Furthermore, make sure you have a website with information that's always current, adds value to any conversation, and changes regularly so there are reasons to return to your site and find new material.

Finally, remember that the National Association of Realtors reports 80 percent of today's real estate transactions start on the internet. So your future business success may depend on making it easier for clients to learn about your services online.

Branding. Recommendations. Communications. Speaking your customer's language. These are the basics of any business, for any product, and for any market. And they're never more important than when sales get shaky. Since realtors may be expecting tough sledding for another few years, it's probably a good direction for anyone in that business to head in today.

FOOD FOR THOUGHT: Whatever your industry, it's always important to find ways to stand out from the crowd.

What's in a (Brand) Name?

In *Romeo and Juliet,* William Shakespeare asked "What's in a name? That which we call a rose by any other name would smell as sweet."

There's a certain truth to what he said, of course, but consider this: There is a debate among Shakespearean scholars as to whether William Shakespeare actually wrote it, or whether his work was really written by a Jewish woman named Aemelia Bassano. Given this was the early 17th century, it was a time when both Jews and women were considered second-class citizens.

So . . . did Shakespeare write it, or did Bassano? Did Shakespeare merely have a better publicist? Or was the name William Shakespeare just a nom de plume used by Bassano to give her more public credibility? And, given that the plays and sonnets exist today in the public domain for all to enjoy, does it really matter anymore?

It matters for historians and purists, of course, though for the rest of us . . . not so much. But what of the respective heirs of William Shakespeare and Aemelia Bassano? Because, while any applicable copyrights ran out long ago, who gets bragging rights?

Far from esoterica, this is a dilemma faced by many businesses worldwide today. The truth is brand names, ownership, and bragging rights can be terribly important. Like your inventory, your brand name has value and needs protection. Just ask Mother Earth Brewery in Vista, California, whose 2011 trademark ruling locked out competitors trying to steal their name.

American courts have ruled a brand's owners must consistently market their name until the trademark is tied to the company in the public mind. If you don't commit to marketing your brand, you become fair game for poaching.

What kind of poaching? Did you know that the words escalator, aspirin, butterscotch, and kerosene were originally brand names? Yet, because their respective owners didn't actively protect these names, they became generic terms with the owners losing their intellectual property rights . . . and *tons* of profits.

Marketing history is littered with hundreds of similar examples with names you take for granted. Scotch tape, zipper . . . there's a long list of trademarked brand names that have lost their legal protection for the reasons noted above.

The lesson? Coasting on your reputation risks someone riding your coattails and stealing your legal rights and profits.

That's why Disney fights so hard anytime someone uses Mickey Mouse to represent a non-Disney item or event without permission.

However, brand names are tricky things. Scrape your knee, reach for a Band-Aid, right? But is it really a Band-Aid . . . or maybe a Curad strip?

As the consumer, odds are you were lured to the store by the marketing efforts (and dollars) of Johnson & Johnson (Band-Aid's owner). Your focus was on the price, benefits, and convenience of the product. The name on the box probably didn't matter to you.

Yet, simultaneously, Curad could have used coupons to capture your sale. And J&J knows if you like that Curad strip you accidentally bought that first time, you'll probably buy Curad again.

If you dislike Curad you'll probably blame Band-Aid. J&J's brand name has become genericized in your mind.

OUCH!

This is the challenge that every creative person, producer, and manufacturer potentially faces at every turn. As my old boss Ron used to say, "A patent or trademark is nice to have, but it's useless unless you're making the effort to enforce it."

Admittedly, I'm not an attorney. I don't even play one on TV. But in my humble opinion, having a trademarked brand name suggests you must act aggressively in order to protect it. Keep a real trademark lawyer on your speed dial, even as you plan to consistently market in any communities you service.

Want more free advice? Watch carefully for anyone using your company's names or images without permission. (Google Search and Google Alerts are good tools for this sort of thing.) Because the more successful you become, the more likely you are to have this problem.

Finally, should you find someone has appropriated your brand name without permission, move fast to claim your rights. Here we might even be able to take a lesson from Johnson & Johnson, who, discovering the term Band-Aid had become generic in the public's mind, was obliged to change their television jingle from, "I am stuck on Band-Aids . . . 'cause Band-Aid's stuck on me" to "I am stuck on Band-Aid Brand. . . "

Obviously, adding the word "Brand" as part of the product's name was deemed helpful to their cause.

The reality is there's no quick and easy solution to this sort of thing, and I'm just a marketing guy who's been on the wrong end of these issues a few times over the past few decades. But I do know that there are some folks out there who will try to steal from your success to line their own pockets without paying you a dime. And I know that if you and your team watch carefully, you'll be able to protect yourself against at least some of the damage.

All of which should ensure your legal rights and profits stay where they belong . . . with you.

FOOD FOR THOUGHT: Should you find someone has "borrowed" your brand name without permission, move fast to reclaim your rights.

Does Marketing with Movies Actually Work?

To announce the launch of my new website (writeawaybooks.com), I'm considering sponsoring a showing of *The Miracle Worker*.

I'm not talking about having an ad on the screen at the local AMC theater, but actually sponsoring movie night of this 1962 classic at senior centers throughout the region.

Seniors are more likely to remember this movie than my daughter's generation. They're also more likely to have a story of their own to tell and the resources to invest in telling it. These are important factors for a company that offers to take Authors from Idea to Manuscript to Marketplace.™

Meaning hosting a movie event like this could (theoretically) enhance our visibility, name recognition, sales opportunities, and perhaps help develop strategic alliances with similarly minded organizations.

An old-fashioned movie night—popcorn and all—has huge potential for expanding awareness of Write Away Books, improving regional goodwill, and ultimately increasing our sales. It also opens the door to a great deal of criticism from the community of those with sight challenges.

But as P.T. Barnum said, "Say anything you like about me, but spell my name right."

Admittedly, the film about Helen Keller and her teacher Anne Sullivan has absolutely nothing to do with a company that helps authors write books. The fact that we've developed what's arguably the world's easiest nonprofit fundraising tool, while laudable, is hardly miraculous.

Even if we use a tagline like "We miraculously make books and dreams come true," it's *still* a bit of a stretch.

Still, the movie's title grabs me as the perfect description of what our little business does. And considering this opportunity makes me wonder why others don't also sponsor movies to exploit their public image.

I know . . . I know . . . so few people go to the movies these days. Competition from Netflix and similar streaming services, as well as from family time, sports events, and the theaters themselves, all conspire against a big turnout of our movie night idea.

Still, it's tempting, as such efforts bring you closer to the grassroots, simultaneously providing tremendous visibility while shutting out the competition for a few hours.

Consider these untapped movie sponsorship opportunities:

- Holiday Inn sponsors . . . *Holiday Inn*
- Dr. Mehmet Oz sponsors . . . *The Wizard of Oz*
- Nike sponsors . . . *Sneakers*

You could almost see the lines forming at the YMCA to see *Can't Stop the Music*—the film about the Village People.

Or a showing of *Casablanca*, supported by Anderson Travel.

Or *Gone with the Wind*, brought to you by Craftsman Fans. Though they'd probably want to make a statement in advance about how *GwTW* isn't politically correct and they don't approve of slavery.

And admittedly, not every film is going to be a good match for every company.

For example, See's Candy probably won't find it advantageous to sponsor the horror flick *Valentine's Day*. Lubriderm probably shouldn't sponsor *Alligator* (also a nasty film).

And my ghoulish sense of humor aside, I can't really see Villa Banfi Chianti and Progresso Fava Beans offering a showing of *Silence of the Lambs*. Anyone who's seen that film understands what I'm talking about.

After over 40 years in the marketing communications world, I've learned about the importance of thinking differently than the other guy. I understand that the average American is bombarded by *so* many marketing messages every day that they can't even see straight after a while.

And I also know that with these communiqués come from every possible direction: the cars we drive, the coffee cups we drink from, and the games we play on our cell phones (to name just a few). This makes it even more important than ever to get noticed and heard above the din.

So with everyone else advertising online, I figure it's worth rolling the dice a little and investing in some one-on-one outreach. Sponsoring a local film means you'll make some real friends, rather than virtual ones, and hopefully share a few laughs along the way.

Laughter, after all, encourages people to like you. And, as I've always said, people buy from those they know, like, and trust.

Which suggests perhaps it's time for clothing manufacturer Hart Schaffner Marx to sponsor a Marx Brothers' festival and get us all into a good mood again.

Or would it be more appropriate for a showing of *The Emperor's New Clothes* down the street from the next candidate debate?

Either way, you're sure to get some tongues wagging and maybe grab a headline or two. That, in turn, should improve your visibility, your sales, and your bottom line.

And *that* is the story we really all came to learn about.

FOOD FOR THOUGHT: Don't just do the same kind of marketing everyone else does. Nobody will be able to tell the difference between you and the other guy.

Nonprofit Branding

You're a Rotten Piece of @#$%^&*(!

D uring the Los Angeles riots of 1992, Rodney King famously asked, "Can we all get along?" Sadly, the answer was—and remains—a resounding "No!"

There's far too much acrimony in the world today, and it's only getting worse. Authors, actors, musicians, and corporations are aggressively pursuing their own activist political agendas, and others are responding accordingly.

Country music fans boycotted the Dixie Chicks for questioning President Trump. Florida's governor punished Disney for daring to question his "Don't Say Gay" legislation. Hobby Lobby is embargoed by progressives, while Levi's is targeted by conservatives.

The list is seemingly endless.

In each case, supporting Group A for humanitarian, economic, religious, or political reasons upsets Group B. Group B, in turn, calls for an economic boycott to hurt anyone who likes Group A.

Sometimes such boycotts work. Because, although most calls for boycotts are bluffs, if Group B is sufficiently angry, organized, and funded, that threat becomes a reality.

And sometimes those realities can be very effective. Consider the fact that today, for the first time in 40 years, I'm buying a childhood favorite: Nestlé's Crunch Bars.

My hiatus was prompted by a college-era boycott on anything Nestlé, due to their unethical practices associated with selling baby formula to Africa's poor in the mid-seventies.

Their policies caused thousands of infant deaths, prompting me to never buy from them until things changed. And though officially ended a few years back, the Nestlé boycott was still alive and well in my mind.

Which is the real challenge with boycotts: They can last for decades in a consumer's mind, even if the original call to action is ancient history.

When organized properly, these powerful tools hit an "offender's" pocketbook to get policies changed.

Did the 2022–23 uproar caused by Fox News's Tucker Carlson over whether M&M's animated characters were wearing proper footwear accomplish anything? Mars Wrigley, M&M's owner, pulled the characters from use as a marketing tool, lest they offend Mr. Carlson and the largest cable news audience in the United States. But who can say what was actually achieved?

Mars Wrigley earns over $20 billion annually, and their pockets are deep enough to survive any negative publicity, rallies, and lost profits ...yet they backed down. Meaning if your pockets aren't that deep, you should watch out for potential boycotts.

Because each time you share your beliefs on social media, you risk irritating customers who disagree with your position. And your customers are more likely today to go onto their own social media accounts and complain about you.

The bottom line: The temporary satisfaction you may get from posting a meme comparing Donald Trump to Adolf Hitler or Hillary Clinton to the Wicked Witch of the West may ultimately pale next to the amount of business you could potentially drive away.

Please don't get me wrong; I'm a great believer in comparing notes and hashing out differences. By all means, debate positions and policies. But remember the potential impacts on your business if you get too aggressive with your own position.

Make every effort to lower the conversation's tenor from shouting to civilized discourse without name-calling. Then, before you start posting conspiracy theories, try not to offend the very people you're attempting to charm into your store.

Finally, a piece of long-forgotten political trivia. Walter Cronkite, for decades America's most trusted news broadcaster, was invited to run for vice president in 1980. He declined, observing: "Everyone loves me today, but it's largely because they don't know my positions on all the issues. If they *did* know my positions, they probably wouldn't like me as much."

We can all learn from him. You want to grow your business. Think how disrespectful political posturing on your part may drive your customers into someone else's arms.

And recognize how long people will willingly sacrifice their favorite things in the name of their own principles.

═══════════════════════════════

FOOD FOR THOUGHT: Watch what you say politically. Customers will willingly sacrifice their favorite things in the name of their own principles.

Are You Ready to Swoop & Scoop?

Shortly after moving to New York City in 1983, I found myself at a party where I knew nobody but the hostess.

Stuck in a corner with another gent who also apparently knew nobody else, I started a conversation by telling him, "My mother has always warned me there are four things you shouldn't talk about with strangers: sex, money, politics, and religion. These are all very personal subjects, and no matter what position you take, you're sure to offend someone."

This fellow considered me for a minute and, with a twinkle in his eye, asked, "Which one should we talk about first?"

Despite that momentary success, I've always leaned toward Mom's philosophy and avoided these delicate subjects.

Still, it's a risk I feel obliged to take once again after recently seeing *The Book of Mormon*. This award-winning Broadway show, written by the developers of television's *South Park*, skewers organized religion in general and the Mormon religion in particular.

Mormonism is one of America's fastest growing religions, so the show pokes a finger into a lot of eyes. And you'd be justified in assuming the folks in Salt Lake City were initially steamed about the whole situation.

Yet by being open to a different type of advertising strategy, the Mormon Church turned a potential public relations disaster into a marketing opportunity.

Imagine thousands of happy theatergoers reading through the program. There, on the latter pages, they encounter three full-page advertisements for the *real* book of Mormon. "You've seen the play. Now read the book," reads one.

Brilliant!

Now if we're being completely candid, I doubt the elders of the Mormon Church wanted to ally themselves to the script's obvious hostility.

Yet the show's nationwide tour provided the Mormon Church with a unique opportunity to promote themselves.

And, to their credit, the church took advantage of it.

Most people are unaware of the many layers of detail needed to build a creative communications success. They look at marketing and assume it happens by opening a magic drawer or buying a box of imprinted pens. In many minds it's based on the luck of being in the right place at the right time.

Admittedly, happenstance can be a factor. However, relying on luck to get a good marketing result is like planning on winning the lottery as your approach toward a successful retirement. Because the fact is, good marketing is equal parts strategy, message, budget, and placement.

Consider, for example, the small manufacturer of custom-flavored ketchup. Premium priced, it's sold at Vons supermarket *right* next to the generic ketchup. Vons highlights their own brand in the local newspaper's sales flyers, lapping up sales based on no other factor than price.

Yet if the upscale ketchup manufacturer places a clever point of sale promotion on the shelf, they can steal a lot of customers who were driven to the store by the competition.

Clever, no?

This is kind of what the Mormon Church has done . . . and quite effectively, I might add. They've allowed the theater to lure in potential customers who read through the program and WHAM!: At the last minute they've stepped in with their very effective messaging.

Because, regardless of what you think about the Mormon religion or the show's irreverence toward it, we should all be able to agree that approaching this potentially derisive audience and saying, in effect, "Hey, let us tell you our side of the story," is inspired.

Taking a tongue in cheek attitude doesn't hurt either.

Of course, we'll never know how successful these image ads were. Yet I'd argue that their advertising placement was smart, their messaging succinct, the budget well spent, and the strategy sound.

Regardless of what you sell, you, too, can learn a lesson here. We all have competitors who are better funded and/or more prominent. However, being clever and willing to think a bit differently could easily position your organization to swoop in and scoop up some business, stealing it from the other guy at the last moment.

And when it comes to closing the deal, that last moment is truly the only one that matters.

Which is why I suggest you remain open-minded when developing your own marketing campaigns. Sure, consider the usual vehicles—Facebook, radio, etc. Then consider the unusual ones . . . because that's probably where success lies.

And if you keep your eyes (and your mind) open to possibilities, you may discover ways to piggyback your message on someone else's efforts . . . just like the Mormon Church did.

After all, scooping up customers and getting them to give you their money is the message preached by the Church of Commerce. For that, let's all give a big "AMEN!"

FOOD FOR THOUGHT: Being clever and willing to think a bit differently could easily position your organization to swoop in and scoop up some business, stealing it from the other guy.

What the Duck Are You Talking About?

The Northern San Diego neighborhood of Rancho Bernardo (also known locally as RB) is a planned community, with a healthy mix of industry, retail, social groups, and the kinds of things one expects in the suburbs.

Late every spring, the RB Business Association (RBBA) holds a fundraiser so they can support local charitable causes. Area residents and businesses are asked to sponsor rubber ducks, signage, and advertising for a windblown race across the lake in a local park.

You'll know it's duck season (not wabbit season) when realtor Patti Hall dons her waterfowl costume and waddles very publicly around town. Patti's a wonderful person with a great sense of humor who's willing to look silly for the larger purpose of helping do good within the community around her.

This race itself is a regular activity on the Fourth of July, and dozens of volunteers fan out in May and June to raise awareness of the event. The only problem is that by July 6 it's largely forgotten, and due to volunteer turnover and a 10-month dormancy, management basically needs to repeatedly resell the duck race every year.

This strikes me as an absurd waste of both potential and momentum, and prompts the question: Why doesn't the RBBA sell event sponsorships year-round?

The way I figure it, there are people who are traveling for July 4 who aren't going to be around to sponsor those ducks. Plus there's been an increasing trend to wait until the last minute to commit to a range of charitable causes, with an eye toward seeing if a better opportunity comes along.

But if you're not going to be there, or your cash flow is tied up for a trip to the Grand Canyon (or wherever), then . . .

Here's something else to consider: Corporate budgets all start at different points on the calendar, and fitting a nonprofit organization's fundraising request into that budget sometimes takes both time and finesse.

Were I king of the forest, I'd be applying for corporate funding in early fall on the assumption that it'll take until June to work through the company's system.

Plus with so many nonprofit groups vying for attention, something must be done to enable a single group to stand out from the crowd a bit more.

Which brings us back to Patti Hall's strategy and commitment. Here's a woman who's found a way to stand out of any crowd, and her outfit's a *great* conversation starter.

Only wearing a duck suit year-round isn't practical, meaning an alternative promotional tool—one suitable to a wider pool of volunteers—may be in order.

Let's be clear here—I'm not talking about handing out coffee mugs, pens, or other items that add to the overhead. Of course, arguably, offering toy ducks wearing t-shirts emblazoned with the RBBA logo to the largest sponsors would be a nice thank-you gift, but that's only for the larger donors.

For the rank-and-file supporters, though, something is needed to reinforce the idea of the race without costing a lot of money.

Fans of the TV show *How I Met Your Mother* probably remember Barney, the unrestrained character played by Neil Patrick Harris. In the seventh season, Barney loses a bet and is forced to wear a rubber duck–imprinted necktie for a year.

My daughter and I watched that show together, and she bought me that same tie with the comment "You're the only one I know who's crazy enough to wear it." It's worth mentioning that she also gave me duck socks and homemade duck cufflinks for birthday and holiday gifts.

I'm sensing a theme here!

I wore this tie to the annual Thanksgiving luncheon put on by the Rancho Bernardo Charitable Foundation. The tie's novelty attracted tremendous attention. Every one of the 400 community leaders in attendance there went out of their way to see my neckwear.

Still, I was stunned when County Supervisor Dave Roberts ascended the dais to speak about what's going on in the world of North San Diego, only to spontaneously give my tie a shout-out.

Now let's connect a few dots:

- RBBA has a rubber duck fundraiser it needs to resell each spring.
- RBBA needs to find ways to stand out from the crowd.
- Rubber duck ties are great conversation starters.
- At $10 (Amazon), rubber duck ties are an inexpensive promotional tool.

Conclusion: Having RBBA sales reps (regardless of gender) regularly wearing rubber duck ties year-round will brand them to the race, initiate conversations about their own businesses, and increase sales opportunities for this charitable event.

It's also sure to expand awareness, publicity opportunities, social media, and all the rest for everyone involved.

It's important to remember that the average American adult is bombarded by *thousands* of marketing messages every 24 hours. This means that, regardless of what you sell, there's a lesson here for your business. Competition for every kind of customer attention is horrific . . . and getting worse.

And if you're like most service businesses, you go hunting for business only when you want more customers, but then slack off when you're too busy.

This is a *huge* mistake! Regardless of your industry or your message, finding gentle ways to develop ongoing visibility provides reasons for people to seek you out, be associated with you, and do business with you. Being able to state categorically that you're involved year-round trying to make the community a better place can only help your business . . . whatever it may be.

Finally, if you're marketing your organization while your competition isn't promoting theirs, you're more likely to get the business. Of course, if the other guy is marketing and you aren't . . . well, you get the point.

Bottom line: It's easier, cheaper, and more effective to remind people you're there, rather than having to completely reeducate them every time you wake up to the need for increasing your sales.

FOOD FOR THOUGHT: It's easier, cheaper, and more effective to remind people you're there, rather than having to completely reeducate them every time you wake up to the need for increasing your sales.

I'm Sick of That Commercial!

B etween cable, DVD, Wii, *Animal Crossing*, and Roku, we've got five remotes in our living room. Being over the age of four, I don't know how to operate any of them.

Yet I couldn't help but notice that the Roku remote has a purple cloth tab sticking out of the bottom, helping it stand out from the crowd of black remotes.

Who cares, right? After all, Roku's not counting on the remote or that purple tab for their marketing efforts. For me, it's just an idle observation . . . so let's not discuss it anymore.

What's *really* important right now are the three copies of the same political campaign postcard that arrived simultaneously in my mailbox yesterday.

Because, while I'm a great believer in repeating your message over the course of a campaign, hitting me multiple times with the exact same message within a few seconds is guaranteed to turn me off . . . not to mention it being a colossal waste of resources.

And, because I'm over the age of four, I'm pretty sure I got the message from the first postcard.

Meanwhile, back on Roku, I discovered a free channel with multiple episodes of a single show. More than most, this channel apparently only exists to sell advertising and make money.

Six minutes in there was a block of five ads, then back to the show. Six minutes later, another five ads . . . and so on.

But there's a wrinkle, because that first block of five ads were all the same spot for a political candidate. The second block of advertising was the same car ad, shown repeatedly. Then came a block of the same ad, five times, for the food bank.

You can see where I'm going with this, right?

Obviously, the station had an obligation to show each ad five times, and they successfully fulfilled that obligation. Yet they did their advertisers no favor.

The fact is I might have stuck around for each of these ads once. However, I don't have the patience for their programming strategy, and by the third time I was in the kitchen getting a snack. Then I went to the bathroom. Then I started thinking about buying from the competition. Finally, I just switched channels.

Doesn't this seem counterproductive to their objectives?

Certainly, I respect their motives (sell advertising, make money). However, the folks who run this channel might want to rethink the way they're actually implementing things.

Because no ad, no matter how persuasive at tugging at your heart strings, is going to sell you something by just droning on. The mere consecutive repetition of the same ad virtually guaranteed the advertisers saw diminishing returns. They, in turn, probably won't be revisiting this station for another contract.

True, good advertising helps close the deal. And success comes from touching your audience from multiple angles so they will remember you when they're finally ready to buy. Productive communications efforts deliver variations of one message, all leading to the same conclusion.

But, in this case the channel on Roku hurt itself. And they could have solved the problem easily if each ad were instead shown once every six minutes. Then there's also a better chance that someone who went to the kitchen for the first round of advertising would see the same commercials in the second round.

Of course, the sponsors aren't blame-free, either. They knew in advance when the ads would run and apparently didn't complain. Yet, if each of them had watched their own commercial five consecutive times (i.e., from the perspective of the viewer), they'd probably have agreed their ad lost its punch over time.

As you're considering your own marketing efforts, take time to consider them from the audience's perspective. Examining your messaging through a customer's eyes before authorizing distribution may make a huge difference in the way your product or service is perceived *and* how much you're able to sell.

Simply put, whether you're spreading the word on TV, social media, or in the mail, distribute your messaging across a longer timeframe. Send the same postcard every few days, or even every couple of weeks. Show the same ad a few minutes apart.

Because I guarantee that monotony-inducing strategies do little to help any sponsor's bottom line. And none of us wants to invest in driving business to the competition.

FOOD FOR THOUGHT: As you're considering your own marketing efforts, take time to consider them from the audience's perspective.

Have You Got Any Grey Poupon?

I f you've ever wondered why it's important to care about your business's reputation, remember what my mother always told me: "Reputations take years to build and can be ruined overnight."

Yup. What people say about your business determines whether or not someone wants to buy from you.

Sounds simple, right? But in these days, when a rumor can literally go around the world faster than you can read this sentence, protecting your reputation needs to be at the top of your mind at all times.

You believe otherwise at your own peril.

Consider a few years back when my (then) teenage daughter was doing the college dance. In the process of attending countless college fairs, my daughter, my bride, and I collected catalogs, pens, and thumb drives from over 260 potential suitors.

Each of these schools offered a smooth sales pitch and an attractive full-color brochure on expensive glossy paper. Many of them gave away branded swag appropriate for college-bound youths. And each of them projected a (hopefully) irresistible image.

My daughter's plan was to sing opera (she succeeded), and we knew we had to get it right the first time. Furthermore, we were determined that our 17-year-old child wouldn't leave school with a bachelor's degree in one hand and a $150,000 promissory note in the other.

The three of us took the next several weeks reviewing these marketing materials, laying them out on the living room floor. We debated and deleted based on geography, community style, religious requirements, political affiliations, and academic demands . . . or lack thereof.

It was a challenging task as we struggled to separate the wheat from the chaff with a target goal of eight applications.

Filtering through those hundreds of similar sales pitches was an interesting experience. And we noticed that throughout the process, there were two school names that kept popping up: Juilliard and Curtis Institute of Music.

Now, coming from New York City, my wife and I knew in advance we'd be hearing about Juilliard. We also knew they have a reputation for having an attitude problem there, and weren't too keen about our daughter attending. At 17, she already had *enough* of an attitude, thank you very much!

But Curtis? We'd never even heard of this Philadelphia-based school. And now that I think of it, I'd (interestingly) never even seen (before or since) any promotional materials about them.

For the uninitiated, Curtis has the lowest acceptance rate of any US university. Besides providing a top-notch education, they are also tuition-free for all 165 (total) enrolled students.

Yes, you read that correctly: 165 students, total, undergraduate and graduate. And if you're looking at their website for more information, don't be surprised if the home page has a statement like: "If you play tuba, don't apply this year; we have one."

Over the years, Curtis has developed a reputation for superior quality, exclusivity, and value, thus needing nothing more than word-of-mouth and a website to market itself. Droves of potential customers would seek them out, and the school would get to choose whom they'll accept.

Curtis even charged significantly more than the other schools on our list to process a student's application, using this as a filter for determining how committed you were to the process.

This is truly an enviable position to be in, no?

It's somewhat akin to the reputation Rolls-Royce has in the automotive industry. Haven't you ever noticed you never see a brochure or a sale for a Rolls-Royce? They don't need the usual tricks of the trade and have such a great reputation that customers seek them out.

In fact, the only time I've ever seen a Rolls in a TV advertisement was in the 1981 commercial when it costarred with a jar of Grey Poupon mustard.

By cultivating an air of exclusivity, Rolls-Royce has been able to leave discounts, commercials, and zero-percent financing promotions to mass-market brands like Toyota.

Regardless of what you sell, you, too, can use an excellent reputation to drive your sales efforts. That's what a consultant friend of mine did after realizing his services were seen as a commodity and his client roster had dwindled to two firms.

To make matters worse, these remaining clients quibbled with him over every invoice, always trying to get him to do work for as close to free as possible.

Then my friend began telling sales prospects he only had room for three new clients. Suddenly folks clamored for his attention, vying to be one of those lucky three.

And, in case you were wondering, my friend recently raised his prices. He's now making more money while working less, and has discovered:

- Potential clients save money to work with him, believing he's worth the investment; and
- More people, feeling he's a winner, seek him out for advice or friendship.

"Someone somewhere will always sell my kind of services for less, so I used my reputation to stand out," he says now.

It's something to consider when examining efforts to grow your own business.

FOOD FOR THOUGHT: Regardless of what you sell, you can use an excellent reputation to drive your sales efforts.

A Better-Late-than-Never Holiday Card

It's March 31, and I *just* mailed my last card from this past holiday season.

My tardiness in getting them all in the mail wasn't done on purpose, nor was it caused by either laziness or lack of interest. The delay was prompted by the typical year-end overload. However, I decided to use the opportunity as a marketing test to see how my audience responded.

When testing direct mail of any type, you need a control group (the way it's traditionally been done) and a test group. So for this experiment, the cards I sent out in mid-December became my control group, and those sent after December 25 became the test group.

Perhaps not surprisingly, many of the cards sent in December were greeted as if they were expected, but not as anything that deserved applause. And whether my cards were handwritten or preprinted didn't seem to make much of a difference. I was checking in amidst the whirl-wind of holiday activity, but there was nothing out of the ordinary about my holiday greetings.

The notes and letters sent in January and February were a different story, though. Whether these notes were handwritten or typed, sent by snail mail or email, almost every one of them received an enthusiastic response, and I stood out from the crowd. I've been hearing back from long-lost friends. Life is good.

Now I'm not suggesting it's profitable to procrastinate. As the sign over my desk says, "PROCRASTINATE LATER." However, it is profit-able to find some way of setting yourself, and your business, apart from the rest of the noise in the marketplace.

My friend Jim gets a jump on the competition each year by send-ing out his Christmas cards and gifts at Thanksgiving. His effort to get noticed before the flood of cards is appreciated by friends and clients alike. My friend Donna sends cards and gifts to celebrate Thanksgiving and skips the Christmas stuff altogether. She, too, seems to engender a higher percentage of goodwill than I do by doing it the old-fashioned way.

I even used to hang around with a group who, every year in July, would throw a "Better Late than Never" Thanksgiving party. It was a big hit and the most-sought-after invitation in town.

All of which suggests there may be a way for you to use the calendar to make your business a bit more noticeable. The realtor I bought my house from sends us a handwritten note on the first day of each new season. My old insurance agent used to send me a birthday card (though my current one doesn't . . . HELLLOOO!—you're missing an opportunity to market yourself to me!).

Don't have access to my birth date? How about sending me and my wife a card for our wedding anniversary? Or one for my dog's birthday? Or a note to celebrate the anniversary of the day you and I started working together?

The point is, if you're doing business with me, you've probably already got information in your files that indicates some date of importance to me. Or else you can easily access this information from public records (like the anniversary of my buying my house, for instance). Then, once you have this date, you can use it as an emotional touchpoint to help you tighten up the relationship you're trying to build with me, your sales prospect/referral source.

Still striking out? Celebrate Labor Day, Independence Day, or Memorial Day. Send out a card celebrating Black History Month or Cinco de Mayo. Or create your own holiday. How about celebrating Dinosaur Destruction Day? Or Toasted Marshmallow Week? Or create a PB&J Festival and send celebratory cards and invitations to the kiddies.

Oh, I know—how about sending out cards wishing people a happy St. Swizzen's Day (there is no such animal) with an invitation to your pub to get your own swizzen (i.e. swizzle) stick?

Bottom line: Use a little imagination. Merely because "This is the way it's always been done" doesn't mean it's the right way, the best way, or the only way to do it. It just means the people doing it that way haven't taken the time and made the effort to find another solution.

FOOD FOR THOUGHT: Finding some way to make yourself appear different in every situation is key to being recognized and gaining future attention and sales.

But for YOU ...
a Special Deal!

Because you're reading the first edition of this book, you get these two bonus columns.

These are the two most popular columns I've ever run, and not a week goes by that I don't get love notes about them ... even years after they originally ran.

Enjoy! I hope you get some genuine value from these ... and all the columns in this book.

Successfully Working from Home

D ecades in a home-based office have taught me some valuable lessons on keeping both sane and productive.

As a public service, and recognizing that most entrepreneurs and independent workers start their career at the kitchen table, I'd like to share these thoughts to help anyone working from home.

1. Always dress as if you were going to work outside the home. It helps keep your mindset in work mode.

2. Follow a regular routine for waking up, drinking coffee, and being at your desk.

3. Work regular hours, but be flexible. If you start early, stop early.

4. Have a dedicated workspace with work-related equipment and supplies.

5. Set ground rules for when kids or others can interrupt you. Don't just leave a sign reading "KEEP OUT" or "I'M WORK-ING" on the door, since after a while others will ignore it.

6. Establish an organizational structure so nothing important escapes your notice. Color-coded spreadsheets are good for that kind of thing.

7. Attend lectures, take classes, and read industry journals to learn about new projects, software, and industry trends.

8. Communicate regularly with coworkers, clients, and super-visors. Let them know when important tasks are finished or you're available for new projects.

9. Join appropriate professional networking groups, like Rotary and the local Chamber of Commerce. They're an important tool for meeting prospecting clients and service providers.

10. Attend and participate in both in-person and online meetings to keep your face in front of people. Don't just communicate via phone, text, or email.

11. Take a full hour for lunch. Don't eat at your desk, but use the time to watch TV, read a book, take a walk, or just let your mind wander.

12. Take breaks from your desk every few hours for a stroll, let the dog get some air and exercise, take a nap, or do laundry. Do it more often if possible, since many studies show that walking for five minutes every half hour can have a huge positive impact on your health.

13. If you're sick, take sick time ... or you're no good to anyone. And as you're getting back to work, be sure to pace yourself. Trust me ... the work will still be there tomorrow.

14. Take time to talk with friends. They'll give you a solid grounding, and provide a point of reference to what's important. Remember the saying, "All work and no play makes Jack a dull boy."

15. Stay positive. People can hear a smile on the phone. A good attitude makes others want to communicate with you, and will improve your overall efficiency.

16. Take advantage of being home so much. Do some baking, organize a closet ... do something for *you.*

17. Now's a good time to catch up on paperwork or phone calls you've been postponing for volunteer projects.

18. *Relax!* Anyone running a business is experiencing similar types of stress. Do your work, but forgive yourself for staring into space periodically. You probably did it at the office, too.

19. End the day with a regular routine telling your brain it's time to shut down. Walk the dog, drink some wine, hug your kids ... or maybe do all three.

20. Don't forget to spend quality time with your spouse or partner. They're helping you turn your idea into reality, so be nice to them. And remember to go out on date nights. Even couples

married many decades can still keep the relationship fresh by not taking each other for granted.

Determine what works best for you, then turn to others for support and insight. Being kind to yourself and those around you minimizes the stress that automatically comes with running any kind of business.

———————————

FOOD FOR THOUGHT: All entrepreneurs have to deal with the same kinds of issues. Don't try to do everything by yourself.

Boardsi: A Scam Geared toward Professionals

The ad seemed genuine enough. Posted on LinkedIn, it offered a portal for paid board of director seats. Intrigued, I scheduled a 20-minute interview.

LinkedIn, for those unfamiliar with it, is *the* place to have a professional profile. It's inhabited by professionals of every stripe, discipline, and industry, and is for business networking only.

So here was this ad from Boardsi, a firm I'd never heard of. But I got busy and had to cancel the meeting . . . plus something just didn't "feel" right.

So I did a bit of research, only to uncover hundreds of posts about what a scam this company is.

Well, you know the old saying about where there's smoke . . .

Apparently, this firm (some argue it's the same company as Exe-cRanks and AdvisoryCloud, though Boardsi's CEO says this is untrue) posts ads like the one I'd seen, offering $30,000 per year or equity to sit on a board. To gain access to their database, you're charged $200 per month . . . and many of the jobs probably don't even exist.

One review after another talked about Boardsi's lack of communication and an unceasing drive by their sales team to separate you from your credit card number.

When I learned this, two old sayings suddenly jumped to mind: John Bridges's "A fool and his money are soon parted" and W.C. Fields's "Never give a sucker an even break."

So I extricated myself from a situation that appears to be unethical and illegal and is unquestionably intolerable.

And though the temptation was to just move on with my life, it struck me that a column like this carries with it a responsibility to alert the public to what seems to be fraudulent behavior.

With an eye toward full disclosure, I will say here that I have heard (twice so far) from Boardsi CEO Martin Rowinski, who insists Boardsi is legitimate. Whether that is true I leave to the individual to do their own research and make up their own mind.

However, in the interests of doing my daily good deed, I'd like to encourage you to be increasingly vigilant about the shysters, scam artists, and other nefarious efforts to separate you from your hard-earned money.

Because whatever business you're in, odds are good there's someone targeting you at this moment with a questionable offer. It may be a "Who's who in your industry?" book, or an award as the best (fill in the blank) in town.

Perhaps not coincidentally, they all seem to have a price point of around $200 in common . . . too little to sue over, but enough (in volume) to net them a tidy sum.

And remember . . . if it sounds too good to be true, it probably is.

FOOD FOR THOUGHT: If it sounds too good to be true, it probably is.

Food for Thought

Smart People Sometimes Do Stupid Things

There's a (questionable) legend that's been going around for decades about Gerber making a huge tactical error. Looking to sell their products in Africa, the story goes that they brought with them the packaging familiar to Western audiences. On the label was a cherubic White infant, the words "Gerber Baby Food," and the flavor of fruit or vegetable that the package contained.

According to this bit of apocrypha, Gerber overlooked the reality that most consumers in Africa couldn't read. Rather, they'd take the image on the label as an indication of what was inside.

Thus, a label with an apple on it would be expected to have apples inside. And a label with a baby on it would be expected to contain pureed baby inside the jar.

Given such circumstances, sales could obviously not be expected to take off. Hence this tale is one of the perennial favorites in the "bad marketing examples" sweepstakes.

Regardless of the veracity of this particular story, though, the fact is smart marketers sometimes do dumb things. Coke prematurely changed its formula. Coors Brewing translated its slogan "Turn it loose" to Spanish, only to realize (too late) it translated as "Suffer from diarrhea."

Swedish firm Electrolux used "Nothing sucks like an Electrolux" as an introduction to the US market. Clairol introduced the Mist Stick in Germany, only to discover (again, too late) that *Mist* is slang for *manure*. And Colgate introduced a toothpaste in France called Cue, the name of a notorious porno magazine.

Then there was the Miami entrepreneur who made thousands of T-shirts for when the Pope visited Mexico. The shirts should have said "Vi El Papa" (I saw the Pope), but instead said "Vi La Papa" (I saw the potato).

Perdue. Pepsi. Parker Pen. The list of such legendary screw-ups is endless, and for my money, you can add GoDaddy's CEO Bob Parsons to the list. Here's the story, straight from *Vanity Fair* (April 5, 2011):

> Thus the man who used racy Super Bowl commercials to create the world's largest website domain hosting company stepped in a pile of ooze by illegally killing a young female elephant.

> Seen (so far) 713,000 times, the gory video brought widespread condemnation from People for the Ethical Treatment of Animals (PETA) and others. Labeling Parsons "The scummiest CEO on earth," PETA very publicly canceled their GoDaddy accounts as tens of thousands followed suit. GoDaddy's bottom line took a considerable hit.

For quite a while, Facebook and Twitter (now rebranded as X) were white hot with chats about how awful Parsons is. The World Wildlife Federation and similar organizations used him as a fundraising tool, while discussing how intelligent elephants are and the importance of treating them respectfully.

Then competitors jumped into the fray, offering to switch domains from GoDaddy (free) and contribute to the World Wildlife Federation, Elephants Without Borders, and similar groups.

Parsons tried to spin the story, noting how many people ate the elephant. But the killing was illegal, and she was at the age to start bearing calves.

And this wasn't GoDaddy's first controversial move. Women popping out of dresses at congressional hearings, NASCAR driver Danica Patrick discussing her beaver . . . all were geared to generating water cooler conversations.

Mr. Parsons obviously lives by the theory that there's no such thing as bad publicity. Maybe he's right. Seeing himself as a latter-day Ernest Hemingway, Mr. Parsons has always figured he can do what he wants with impunity, and the hit he took from this particular episode didn't last long.

Yet in these days of political correctness, one must take customer sensibilities into account. Customers *do* care how their vendors act, and show their displeasure by moving their business elsewhere.

Just as Mr. Trump and Mr. Musk (of political and Twitter infamy, respectively) have learned, Mr. Parsons may also one day understand that there *is* such a thing as bad publicity and going too far ... even when editors spell your name properly.

And if you do something dumb, sometimes you should tuck your tail between your legs, apologize, and hope you'll be forgiven.

════════════════════════════

FOOD FOR THOUGHT: In these days of political correctness, one must take customer sensibilities into account. Customers *do* care how their vendors act, and show their displeasure by moving their business elsewhere.

Rob Weinberg Is Missing!

They haven't yet sent out the St. Bernards (with their casks of brandy!). However, last week it came close.

Regular readers of my column know my Panama hat helps me stand out of any crowd. After wearing one for the past 30 years, the hat and I are one in many minds, and it's become my trademark.

Standout image plus consistent usage equals solid branding, right?

Yet last week the question arose: Is it possible to over-brand oneself?

For five and a half years I've belonged to a nonprofit business support group. For the past four years I've been on their board of directors.

I actively participate in monthly meetings and am *anything* but a wallflower. And, since we're inside, I don't wear my hat. Rather, it sits on the table in front of me.

At last week's meeting, the chair called for my committee report . . . and didn't see me. "Where did he go?" she asked. Everyone in the room looked around for me.

Sans hat, I'd become invisible. The moment I put it on and stood up, everyone recognized me and applauded.

No, I'm *not* making this up.

And I'll confess that this isn't the first time this sort of thing has happened. Without the hat I've had family members unable to find me at Costco and been yelled at by chamber of commerce executives. Said one, "How can I introduce you as 'The Man with the Hat, when you're *not* wearing your hat?!'"

Fair point.

Wearing one style of hat most waking hours has helped brand me with a particular image. As a marketing professional, that has always been my goal. And while some call it an expensive hobby, I prefer to see it as an investment in my own marketing.

And over time, the hat has become an extension of my personality. It's the embodiment of my brand, and has been successfully woven into my logo and all communications materials.

With the hat, I've been greeted by strangers and recognized months after I'd spoken at conferences. It's encouraged strangers to come over to say hello at the supermarket, Starbucks, or on the street. And it virtually guarantees that readers will approach to praise or berate me about something I've written recently.

Thus the hat and I are woven together in the public imagination. The choice of whether to wear it was apparently decided a *long* time ago.

But last week's meeting delivered incontrovertible proof: There's also a downside to all this visibility and, dare I say it, notoriety. Because, with increasing frequency, when I show up someplace *without* my hat in its proper place, people just don't recognize me anymore.

And so the question remains: Is there such a thing as too much branding?

After considerable thought on this issue, I've concluded the answer is: No, it's not possible to over-brand.

There's absolutely no downside to any individual or business providing a uniform message and image. More than 40 years of professional experience tells me a business can't apply too much effort to branding itself, provided the message and image are consistent.

Because there's a reason that Coca-Cola spends billions of dollars, year after year, drilling their image into your head. McDonald's, Proctor & Gamble, Apple, and the rest of the gang all do the same.

Why? They need to protect the value and equity built into their respective brands. It's important if they want any hope of selling more stuff and growing the bottom line.

So why do people *not* see me? It's obviously the inconsistency on my part—not wearing my brand (i.e. my hat) all the time—that causes the problem.

Now let's take a look at *your* business. Regardless of what you sell or do, do you have a single consistent image (colors, font, tagline, signage, etc.) presented to the public? Does it carry through all of your marketing materials—website, social media, business cards, collateral, and the like?

And, at the risk of belaboring the point, are you "wearing" your brand everyplace, night and day?

Because an organization with 15 brochures, each with different colors, fonts, and types of borders, isn't creative; it's disjointed. Meaning if you're like so many organizations (both for-profit and nonprofit) and you're using multiple identifying images and color palettes, you're probably confusing people.

Along the same lines, you should also find the tone that suits your firm and your audience and keep that consistent across all platforms, too. Because, once again, if you're silly on your website and morose on your social media, visitors will be unclear that they're talking to the same people.

In short, find one image, message, and tone to represent you, then make sure it appears everyplace. I know I've said it before—and I'll say it again—because this is a message that bears repeating.

Finally, know the name of your font family and the PMS colors (or HEX on your website) that you're working with. Note these details in your business or marketing plan, to help ensure what's created next year matches what you're developing today.

Oh, and those graphics, photos, and illustrations you're showing on the website? Don't be afraid to repurpose them in collateral, social media, and elsewhere. It'll help reinforce your story in a customer's mind.

Creating consistent branding isn't easy, nor should the process be rushed. But, if done properly, you, too, may soon have strangers approaching you at parties saying, "I know who you are."

FOOD FOR THOUGHT: Find one image, message, and tone to represent your organization, then make sure it appears everyplace.

And Now . . . a Moment of Introspection

'***ve never been one to focus on my age. Inside I'm still 25 (though my
back has other ideas), so why make a fuss about another day on the
calendar?

However, Thursday's my 65th birthday. It's waiting for me like a
cougar, striking when the time is right. It's unavoidable.

Admittedly, it's not a surprise. For months I've been receiving a
steady stream of Medicare "educational" mailers from one "free" service
after another. Their cumulative message has been crystal clear: "There's
a freight train bearing down on you, and there's *nothing* you can do to
get out of the way."

CRAP! Sixty-five is for *old* people, and I'm vibrant, energetic, and
ready to hit the ground running every morning. "Screw you and your
Medicare!" I think, unwilling to give in to the forces of nature.

The fact is that, given the chance, I'd have ignored the whole mess,
celebrating over a quiet dinner with my bride. But she and my daughter
prevailed upon me to acknowledge this year with a few close friends.

And stepping back, the entire discussion has presented me with a
dilemma. Like Jack Benny, I could eternally proclaim I'm 39. Or I could
just celebrate the anniversary of my 25th birthday.

But given that the crowd I hang around with is more than likely
to call "Bullshit!" I'm guessing it wouldn't work. Besides, I've known
most of my friends longer than 25 years.

As a Rotarian, I am forced to ask, "Is it the truth?" sigh, and know
that none of those solutions will work. I'm 65 and must deal with that
milestone.

As Robin Williams said: "Reality . . . what a concept."

Turning 65 is a perfect time to take stock in yourself and see if you've
accomplished what you wanted to with your life. If you have, it's a good
opportunity to make travel plans and ease out of the rat race.

Only I haven't accomplished what I set out to do professionally. I've spent years giving my advice away for little or no money. Now I find myself yearning for a few solid financial years before I can afford to even think about retiring.

This, it would appear, is my last chance to make it big.

And like my business's annual marketing plan, I see this as the moment to find doors I want to open and people I wish to meet. It's forcing me to be completely honest about my goals and how I want to get there.

The fact is, acknowledging the reality of my 65th birthday provides me with a wonderful chance to review strategies for this next chapter of my life, family, and career. Which is why I'm now actively replacing efforts that bore me with new challenges and implementing long-considered actions with an eye toward a more interesting tomorrow.

Writing this book was one of the items on that list.

Reviewing my track record to date, I see a wealth of experience and talent aching for the right outlet. It's time to recognize what I deserve, rather than being someone who regularly settles for good enough.

Which explains why I've joined forces with a friend to launch a new business, which you'll find at writeawaybooks.com. We've found a niche, started bringing in customers, and merged our talents to create something with exciting long-term potential. He sees it as our retirement fund, and I tend to agree.

Surrounded by family, friends, supporters, and fans, I'm determined to make this a launching point for years of hard-charging creativity, strategic planning, and marketing solutions bridging traditional and digital media. I'm going to make sure we're surrounded by talented, hardworking people who, above all, know how to have fun.

So I say to *hell* with self-pity and feeling downtrodden . . . I've got work to do! I'll see you in 5 or 10 years, and we can talk about retirement and relaxing then!

FOOD FOR THOUGHT: Turning 65 is a perfect time to take stock in yourself and see if you've accomplished what you wanted to with your life.

Food for Thought—A Summary

BRANDING

1. The best reason for advertising today is the sale you'll make tomorrow. There is always a tomorrow to prepare for, more competition coming down the road, and seeds that need to be planted to grow your bottom line.

2. The average American adult is exposed to roughly 10,000 marketing messages every 24 hours. Any business hoping to break through that noise had better have a good strategy.

3. Consistency across marketing platforms is critical, and the criteria you're using for your overall branding needs to be used by every team of writers and designers to ensure your look and tone remain in place at every level.

4. No business, individual, or nonprofit *ever* got into trouble by having consistent branding.

5. Your company name speaks volumes about you, your ego, your business's personality, your customer, and your product line. Change your company name if you think there's a benefit to the exercise.

6. Use the opportunity when rebranding your business or nonprofit to introduce new services and products. Use every communications tool at your disposal, and make as big a splash as possible.

7. If someone's feeding their ego, naming the company after themselves makes perfect sense. However, those wishing to actually sell stuff should rethink that strategy.

8. Breathing life into a fictional representative increases chances a business will be remembered when it comes time for someone to make a purchase.

9. There's never a downside to consistent and clever promotion of your business.

10. How do you get someone to pay you lots of money and willingly promote your business?

11. Find a symbol to represent your brand. Present it to your audience. Repeat daily.

12. Build in extra time to double-check your work for mistakes and you'll appear more professional.

13. Brand your own company name on your business emails. It's easy, it's smart, and it's potentially lucrative.

14. Remember how you'd like to be treated . . . and pay it forward.

PERSONAL BRANDING

1. People buy from people they know, like, and trust.

2. You should *always* be selling yourself! And remember what Mom said: "You only get one chance at making a first impression."

3. Making yourself memorable in little ways may open some big doors for your success.

4. You'll build long-term quality relationships by being honest about who you are and what value you bring to the conversation.

5. Thinking a little differently has the potential to help you expand your audience for about the same cost as doing the same old, same old.

6. Hard work, dedication, good quality, fair pricing, a solid communications strategy, and intelligent messaging can be combined to help *you* live happily ever after.

7. You're always selling yourself to clients, and that means personality, grooming, clothing, and style.

8. Just looking like everyone else is a guarantee you'll be forgotten.

9. Wearing your name badge on the right side makes it easier to initiate a business conversation.

10. A heart attack or a tax audit is a crisis. Everything else in life is a situation you just have to deal with.

11. If you don't make a good presentation for yourself with what you do professionally, don't expect anyone else to hire you.

12. Many would-be customers think a salesperson with facial hair is shifty or untrustworthy. Being clean-shaven invariably improves your chances of making the sale.

13. Job seekers are advised to dress nicely, have a professional-looking resume, and be prompt for any meetings. For me, add speaking well to the list.

BUSINESS BRANDING

1. There is *no* downside to having a consistent company image throughout your marketing materials. It's something that people who are serious about their business can't afford to ignore.

2. If your business makes a mistake, acknowledge it publicly, apologize, and find some way to quickly make amends . . . then move on.

3. The company's reputation was worth $23 billion in goodwill alone. Then greed, stupidity, and bad management guaranteed it was all lost . . . virtually overnight!

4. Naming a business can be tricky, easily going down the wrong path. Ego, bad taste, politics, and plain old stupidity can all come into play.

5. You're usually better off hiring specialists for particular services, enabling you to focus on what you do best.

6. Know your audience, your message, and your unique features. Together, they should lead you toward a brilliant tagline.

7. A new image for your organization may allow you to clarify your message and reintroduce yourself to people so used to you that they don't even see you anymore.

8. I know there are bugs, mice, or whatever in every commercial kitchen. But when I'm out for either a social or business event, I don't need to be reminded about it.

9. Don't try to create a quality tagline in a vacuum, as doing so virtually guarantees mediocrity.

10. The right image can really get your phones ringing.

11. Creating a personality for your business, and systematically inserting it into all your communications materials, is virtually a guarantee of a fatter bottom line.

12. A reputation for limited availability drives up desirability.

13. Being difficult is the *last* message you want possible customers to come away with before they've even gotten in your front door.

14. Make it as easy as possible for customers to give you their money.

15. Whatever your industry, it's always important to find ways to stand out from the crowd.

16. Should you find someone has "borrowed" your brand name without permission, move fast to reclaim your rights.

17. Don't just do the same kind of marketing everyone else does. Nobody will be able to tell the difference between you and the other guy.

NONPROFIT BRANDING

1. Watch what you say politically. Customers will willingly sacrifice their favorite things in the name of their own principles.

2. Being clever and willing to think a bit differently could easily position your organization to swoop in and scoop up some business, stealing it from the other guy.

3. It's easier, cheaper, and more effective to remind people you're there, rather than having to completely reeducate them every time you wake up to the need for increasing your sales.

4. As you're considering your own marketing efforts, take time to consider them from the audience's perspective.

5. Regardless of what you sell, you can use an excellent reputation to drive your sales efforts.

6. Finding some way to make yourself appear different in every situation is key to being recognized and gaining future attention and sales.

Bonus Branding

1. All entrepreneurs have to deal with the same kinds of issues. Don't try to do everything by yourself.

2. If it sounds too good to be true, it probably is.

Food for Thought

1. In these days of political correctness, one must take customer sensibilities into account. Customers *do* care how their vendors act, and show their displeasure by moving their business elsewhere.

2. Find one image, message, and tone to represent your organization, then make sure it appears everyplace.

3. Turning 65 is a perfect time to take stock in yourself and see if you've accomplished what you wanted to with your life.

Mr. Marketing is available for coaching, consulting, speaking, conferences, and kids' parties. Contact him with your own marketing challenges at www.marketbuilding.com.

www.ingramcontent.com/pod-product-compliance
Lightning Source LLC
Chambersburg PA
CBHW060515130626
46553CB00002B/504